Madison Hydroplane Heritage

Fred Farley
Ron Harsin

Editor: Phyllis Klucinec

Bristol Fashion Publications, Inc.
Harrisburg, Pennsylvania

Madison -- Hydroplane Heritage - Fred Farley & Ron Harsin

Published by Bristol Fashion Publications, Inc.

Copyright © 2003 by Fred Farley & Ron Harsin.
All rights reserved.

No part of this book may be reproduced or used in any form or by any means-graphic, electronic, mechanical, including photocopying, recording, taping or information storage and retrieval systems-without written permission of the publisher.

BRISTOL FASHION PUBLICATIONS AND THE AUTHOR HAVE MADE EVERY EFFORT TO ENSURE THE ACCURACY OF THE INFORMATION PROVIDED IN THIS BOOK BUT ASSUMES NO LIABILITY WHATSOEVER FOR SAID INFORMATION OR THE CONSEQUENCES OF USING THE INFORMATION PROVIDED IN THIS BOOK.

ISBN: 1-892216-48-5
LCCN: 2003109485

Cover Design by: John P. Kaufman

Madison -- Hydroplane Heritage - Fred Farley & Ron Harsin

Acknowledgements

The authors are indebted to all who
helped make this book a reality.

David Greene and Philip Haldeman, both of the APBA Unlimited Historical Committee, for their editorial assistance in the preparation of portions of this book.

Special thanks to everyone who allowed us to use their photos and art designs, especially Rich Ormbrek, Ed Krupinski, Bob Carver, Ky Yarling, Jack Lowe, Judy Fisk, Dale Wilson, The Madison Courier and Hydro-Prop.

Thank you to our families for enduring all the hours while we worked on this book.

To the many people who helped in so many ways. Their names are too numerous to mention, but to all of you...

THANK YOU !!

Photographs

Rich Ormbrek, Bob Carver, Ed Krupinski, Denny Jackson, Judy Fisk, Danny McKeand, Ky Yarling, Fred Farley, Bruce McKim, Cary Toleman, Morris Rosenfeld, Bob Teklinski, David Taylor, Dale Wilson, James V. Carroll, Jack Lowe, Jim Lilly (Graphic Designs), Ron Harsin, Bernie Schwartz, Fred Has, Bill Osborne, David Johnson, Matt Sontag, Casper Hydroplane Models, Bruce McKim, John Knobel, Phil Kunz, George Davis, Bob Talinski, Bernie Schwartz. Brian Grant, Hydro-Prop, Tri-City Herald, The Hydroplane and Race Boat Museum, The Madison Courier, Alan Lagervall, Rusty Neff, Brian Grant, Chuck Moore and Cindy Moore.

All photos used by permission.

Many of the photographs in this book are reproduced from historical archives and, therefore, the quality varies widely throughout. We have reproduced all the photographs, using the latest techniques, in order to match the original photographs as closely as possible.

Madison -- Hydroplane Heritage - Fred Farley & Ron Harsin

Dedicated to

The July 4, 1971 MISS MADISON Crew
Jim McCormick, Tony Steinhardt, Dave Stewart, Bob Humphrey, Keith Hand and Russ Willey. Along with Special Consultants Harry Volpi and Everett Adams.

Madison -- Hydroplane Heritage - Fred Farley & Ron Harsin

Madison -- Hydroplane Heritage - Fred Farley & Ron Harsin

Table of Contents

Photo Credits   Page 4

Preview   Page 9

Chapter One   Page 11
    History Of The Gold Cup

Chapter Two   Page 31
    History Of Hydroplane Racing

Chapter Three   Page 39
    Gone But Not Forgotten

Chapter Four   Page 89
    Madison, Indiana

Chapter Five   Page 103
    History of Hydroplane Racing in Madison, Indiana

Chapter Six   Page 135
    History of MISS MADISON

Chapter Seven   Page 169
    "Madison" The Movie

Chapter Eight Page 201
The 1971 Madison Gold Cup Race

Chapter Nine Page 257
More Madison Regatta

Chapter Ten Page 275
Current Hydroplanes

About The Authors Page 327

Preview

MISS MADISON, 1971

On July 4, 1971, the community-owned hydroplane, MISS MADISON and driver, Jim McCormick, made their run at immortality before 110,000 partisan fans on the Ohio River in Madison, Indiana.

The right to run the 1971 Gold Cup in Madison was nearly lost. Since 1963, the race had been awarded to the city with the highest financial bid rather than to the yacht club of the last winning boat as was the previous custom.

Through a technicality and a misunderstanding, Madison's smaller-than-usual bid for the race was the only one submitted in time.

Madison -- Hydroplane Heritage - *Fred Farley & Ron Harsin*

In 1971, Madison had a population of 13,000. Never before had the Gold Cup been run in such small a town.

Down to their last Allison engine, having blown the other in trials, the aging, under-financed MISS MADISON and Jim McCormick, ran like never before.

This book focuses on the story of that 1971 Gold Cup Race along with the rich heritage of Gold Cup Racing throughout the years.

We invite you to visit our hometown of Madison, Indiana. Come for the 4th of July regatta, when the Madison Hydroplane races are run each year, but also stop back throughout the year to see our quiet town.

Our town takes great pride in its historical setting, architecture and slow river town lifestyle. Whether searching for the excitement of the hydroplane races or spending some quiet time browsing the shops for antiques, Madison offers both. It is truly one of the finest tourist locations in the midwest.

Our doors are always open.

Fred Farley & Ron Harsin

Madison -- Hydroplane Heritage - Fred Farley & Ron Harsin

Chapter One
History Of The Gold Cup

The Current Gold Cup Trophy

The Hydro-Prop/American Power Boat Association (APBA) offers the oldest and most prestigious trophy in hydroplane racing.

This crown jewel of racing is called the Gold Cup.

Affectionately referred to as the "Old Urn", it was

created in 1904, by Tiffany's for a total cost of $900.

First presented in 1904, the trophy has been given annually to the winning hydroplane driver and crew in the Unlimited Hydroplane Gold Cup race.

This trophy, has been presented throughout the years to the sportsmen daring enough to win it.

A Brief History of the Gold Cup Race

The APBA Gold Cup is to power boat racing what the Super Bowl is to football, the Kentucky Derby is to horse racing, the World Series is to baseball and the Indianapolis 500 is to auto racing.

Officially known as the "American Power Boat Association Challenge Cup," it is the ultimate prize that every competitor strives to win at least once.

The Gold Cup's long and fascinating history is one of the great of sports stories. A definitive history of the "Golden Goblet" has yet to be written but would fill many volumes with highlights too numerous to mention here.

The very first Gold Cup race took place in June 1904 on the Hudson River in New York. In those days, the boats plowed through the water rather than skimming over the surface. The winning boat, the STANDARD, owned and driven by Carl Riotte, averaged just over 23 miles per hour. Measuring 59 feet in length with an 8-1/2-foot beam, the craft used a 110-horsepower Standard motor that resembled a miniature steam engine with its steel columns and open frame.

For the first and only time in Gold Cup history, two races were run in the same calendar year. VINGT-ET-UN II, a displacement boat, driven by Willis Kilmer, won the second Gold Cup in September 1904 using a Simplex engine for power. Kilmer's best heat was just over 25 miles per hour.

Madison -- Hydroplane Heritage - Fred Farley & Ron Harsin

STANDARD - The first Gold Cup winner in 1904.

Starting in 1905, a handicap system was utilized which took into account each boat's power and size. The use of this system enabled CHIP, owned and driven by Jonathon Wainwright, to win on corrected time of about 15 miles per hour even though CHIP was the next-to-slowest boat in the fleet.

Protests from losing entrants resulted in scrapping the controversial handicapping system after 1907. Beginning in 1908, the Gold Cup was a "wide open" race. E.J. Schroeder's DIXIE II captured the cup that year and posted a fastest heat speed of over 30 miles per hour.

The first hydroplane hull to win the Gold Cup was MIT II in 1911 with J.H. Hayden at the wheel. The hydroplanes with their underside "steps" and their ability to plane over the surface of the water spelled the end of the displacement hull era.

The first Gold Cup race to be run on the Detroit River was in 1916. This was by virtue of the community-owned MISS DETROIT winning the Cup in 1915 on Manhasset Bay in upstate New York, earning the right to defend it on home waters.

MISS DETROIT was a single-step hydroplane, equipped with a 250-horsepower Sterling engine. The designer was the distinguished Christopher Columbus Smith of ChrisCraft fame. As things developed, MISS DETROIT's debut was almost an unmitigated disaster.

Madison -- Hydroplane Heritage - *Fred Farley & Ron Harsin*

Scheduled to pilot the Motor City entry in the big race was a prominent Detroit yachtsman who shall remain forever nameless. As the countdown for the first heat got under way, MISS DETROIT's driver could not be found. A crewmember named Johnny Milot offered to step in as relief pilot.

Milot did not have time to put on protective gear. He jumped into the cockpit along side riding mechanic Jack Beebe and headed for the race course.

Being unfamiliar with the course layout, Milot followed the other boats around the buoys for the first few laps. The water was very rough and Johnny endured a terrific pounding. By the end of the heat, Beebe was driving after Milot had succumbed to seasickness. but by some miracle, they had managed to finish in first-place.

At the end of the race, the heroes of the day were Johnny Milot and Jack Beebe.

MISS DETROIT had won the Gold Cup and a racing dynasty had begun.

In the years that followed, Detroit displaced New York as the Boat Racing Capital of North America.

Beginning with the 1917 Gold Cup in Minneapolis, Gar Wood, the sport's first superstar, rose to prominence. Named after two U.S. Presidents, Garfield Arthur Wood seemingly became the personification of power boat competition in the eyes of the world. He won the 1917 race at the wheel of MISS DETROIT II. This was Wood's first of five consecutive victories as a driver in "the race of races."

In 1920, at the wheel of his twin Smith-Liberty-powered MISS AMERICA, Wood averaged a phenomenal 70.412 miles per hour in the 30-mile final heat on a 5-mile course. The record would stand until 1946.

In the 1921 Gold Cup, Gar was simply unbeatable and made a shambles of the opposition.

For the next two decades, Gold Cup racing was restricted, supposedly for safety, but obviously to stop Gar

Madison -- Hydroplane Heritage - Fred Farley & Ron Harsin

Wood's domination and put the sport into the range of more pocketbooks than previously. Hydroplane hulls were outlawed and the engine size was limited to 625 cubic inches. The hulls were re-admitted in 1929 and the cubic inch displacement was eventually raised to 732.

A field of thirteen "gentlemen's runabouts" appeared in the 1922 Gold Cup at Detroit. The winner was Jesse Vincent in PACKARD CHRISCRAFT with a 90-mile race average of 40.253. The race also marked the debut of the Packard Gold Cup engine, which would dominate for the next fifteen years.

One of the more bizarre chapters in Detroit Gold Cup history occurred at the 1924 contest. Canadian sportsman Harry Greening had apparently won with his RAINBOW IV, which was seen by some as being a hydroplane rather than a displacement hull. The craft's bottom was of lapstrake construction, which was technically permitted by the rules.

The APBA decided, however, that the strakes had been installed for the express purpose of achieving a hydroplane effect. In other words, Greening had followed the letter of the rules but not the spirit. As a result, RAINBOW IV was disqualified and Caleb Bragg's BABY BOOTLEGGER was moved from an overall second to first position.

Outraged, Greening returned to Canada and never raced for the Gold Cup again.

The most prominent Gold Cup boat of the 1930s was EL LAGARTO, owned and driven by George Reis of Lake George, New York. This boat became the cup's first three-time consecutive winning hull in 1933-34-35. In 1933, "The Leaping Lizard," the nickname for EL LAGARTO, turned the fastest heat (60.866) since the cubic inch piston displacement limitation of 1922.

The first Gold Cup victory by a three-point hydroplane occurred in 1939.

Madison -- Hydroplane Heritage - Fred Farley & Ron Harsin

EL LAGARTO - First three time Gold Cup winner.

    Unlike the step hydroplanes, the three-pointers rode on the tips of two pontoon-like running surfaces called sponsons and a completely submerged propeller. (Not until the late 1940s would the boats start to "propride.") The concept would forever alter the course of competitive power boating.

MERCURY

    MY SIN, a product of the famed Ventnor Boat Works of Ventnor, New Jersey, won all three heats of the 1939 race at Detroit with owner Guy Simmons driving. The other three-pointers in attendance were Bill Cantrell's WHY WORRY,

Lou Fageol's SO-LONG, Marion Cooper's MERCURY and George Davis's HERMES IV.

In 1936, the Ventnor company popularized the three-point design by introducing MISS MANTEO II, a successful 225 Cubic Inch Class hydroplane with vestigial sponsons.

MY SIN repeated as Gold Cup winner in 1941 and again in 1946 as Guy Lombardo's TEMPO VI.

TEMPO IV

After time out for World War II, Gold Cup racing resumed with a rejuvenated format in evidence. The 732 cubic inch piston displacement limitation was abandoned. The introduction of converted Allison and Rolls-Royce Merlin aircraft engines, developed for the war effort, produced new enthusiasm for America's premier power boat racing event.

Although the 1946 race went to the Miller-powered TEMPO VI, Dan Arena's MISS GOLDEN GATE III, running an Allison V-12, raised the Gold Cup lap record to over 77 miles per hour on a 3-mile course.

A two-step Allison-powered craft, the John Hacker-designed MY SWEETIE, raised the 30-mile Gold Cup heat record to 78.645 in 1949 with "Wild Bill" Cantrell driving. This was only a few years after a speed in excess of 70 miles per hour was considered almost "impossible."

During the first half of the 20th Century, no yacht club boat from west of the Mississippi River was ever victorious.

All of that changed in 1950 when SLO-MO-SHUN IV from Seattle finally turned the trick at Detroit. SLO-MO owner Stan Sayres, driver/designer Ted Jones and builder Anchor Jensen thoroughly debunked the well-publicized impression that three-point suspension hulls become hopelessly uncontrollable at racing speeds--especially in the corners.

MY SWEETIE

SLO-MO IV wasn't the first hydroplane to "prop-ride" on a semi-submerged propeller. Jack Schafer's SUCH CRUST II and Morlan Visel's HURRICANE IV had both experimented along those lines. But SLO-MO-SHUN IV was the first craft to reap championship results in the application of the concept. The days when a hydroplane could win with a fully submerged propeller were numbered.

For the next two decades, the boats had to use a SLO-MO-type design or they simply weren't competitive. Overnight, competition speeds of over 100 miles per hour and straightaway speeds of over 150 were commonplace.

When Sayres was presented with the Gold Cup, following his 1950 Motor City triumph, the cynics wagged that the Cup was "only being loaned" to him.

The "loan" proved to be of long duration as Sayres went on to become the first five-time consecutive winning owner of power boating's Holy Grail.

Sayres also introduced Gold Cup racing to the Pacific Northwest. Not again until 1956 would another Gold Cup contest be staged on the Detroit River.

For pure boat racing, it's hard to top the classic 1954

Gold Cup in Seattle, Washington. Indeed, boats ran head-to-head with each other all day on that memorable August 7.

SLO-MO-SHUN V, driven by Lou Fageol, finished first in all three 30-mile heats. However, Lou had to win them the hard way, especially in Heat Two, when SLO-MO-SHUN V, SLO-MO-SHUN IV and MISS U.S. shared the same roostertail for seven of the eight laps.

All of the Gold Cup winners from 1947 to 1953 had used Allison power. SLO-MO-SHUN V was the first boat to achieve competitive results with a Rolls-Royce Merlin engine. The Rolls was more powerful than the Allison but more temperamental.

SLO-MO-SHUN V

Lee Schoenith and GALE V from Detroit finally broke the Seattle Yacht Club's five-year monopoly of the Gold Cup in 1955. GALE V won a disputed decision over Bill Muncey and MISS THRIFTWAY, which involved Bonus points and 4.536 seconds in total elapsed time.

Defending champion Fageol turned a complete backward somersault at 165 miles per hour with SLO-MO-SHUN V, while attempting to qualify for the 1955 race.

For sheer acrimony, nothing tops the protest-ridden 1956 Gold Cup in Detroit, which took 85 days to settle. MISS THRIFTWAY and Muncey were eventually declared the winners and the race went back to Seattle for 1957. All this after the cup had initially been presented to the Detroit-based MISS PEPSI and Chuck Thompson.

Following, and as a result of the 1956 Gold Cup, the Unlimited Racing Commission (now HYDRO-PROP, Inc.) was formed to administer Unlimited Hydroplane activity, instead of the Inboard Racing Commission. All but nominal ties with the parent, American Power Boat Association were severed.

Edgar Kaiser's HAWAII KAI III, designed by Ted Jones, was arguably the greatest race boat of the 1950s. With Jack Regas driving, the KAI won five races in a row and the National High Point Championship. He raised the mile straightaway record from 178 to 187 miles per hour in 1957.

HAWAII KAI III

Following a brief retirement, Regas and HAWAII KAI III came back to save the Gold Cup for Seattle in 1958. This was after the Bill Muncey-chauffeured MISS THRIFTWAY lost her rudder and crashed into a U.S. Coast Guard utility boat at the start of Heat 2-A.

The KAI had her work cut out for her that year. The MAVERICK and driver Bill Stead, who represented the Lake

Madison -- Hydroplane Heritage - *Fred Farley & Ron Harsin*

Mead Yacht Club of Las Vegas, Nevada, had won their two most recent races in 1958 and qualified fastest with a Gold Cup record of 119.956 for three laps around the Lake Washington 3-mile course.

But on race day, August 10, HAWAII KAI III rose to the challenge and beat MAVERICK hands down. This guaranteed a Gold Cup race for Seattle in 1959 as well.

For the first and only time in its history, the APBA Gold Cup was declared "No Contest" in 1960. The Lake Mead Yacht Club had won the right to host the race, following MAVERICK's victory in the 1959 renewal. But high winds churned the lake into an unraceable froth after the completion of only one preliminary heat.

It took three days of delays, but the 1961 Gold Cup was finally completed. Bill Muncey and MISS CENTURY 21 emerged victorious in the only Gold Cup race ever run on Pyramid Lake, near Reno, Nevada. Without winning a heat MISS CENTURY 21 posted three second-place finishes for a total of 900 points; Don Wilson and MISS U.S. I had two first-places and a "Did Not Finish" for a total of 800 points.

Starting in 1963, the Gold Cup race location was determined by the city with the highest financial bid, rather than by the yacht club of the winning boat. The race format was also changed from three heats of 30 miles to four heats of 15 miles. (The current Gold Cup format calls for two heats of 7-1/2 miles and three heats of 12-1/2 miles.)

The high bid in 1963 was by Detroit. In the years since, more Gold Cups have been run on the Detroit River than any other location. Since 1990, all Gold Cup races have been contested in the Motor City.

Ron Musson and MISS BARDAHL established a Gold Cup dynasty in 1963 for owner Ole Bardahl. This was after a battle with second-place Bill Cantrell in GALE V. Musson went on to repeat as Gold Cup winner in 1964 and 1965.

When Musson was fatally injured in the 1966

President's Cup at Washington, D.C., new MISS BARDAHL driver, Billy Schumacher, picked up where Ron had left off. with victories of his own in 1967 and 1968.

1965 MISS BARDAHL

1968 MISS BARDAHL

After seven years, MISS BUDWEISER gave owner Bernie Little, his first Gold Cup in 1969 on San Diego's Mission Bay. MISS BUDWEISER pilot, Bill Sterett, had to battle rival Dean Chenoweth and MYR'S SPECIAL in 1969 not only for the Gold Cup but also for the National High Point Championship.

Thirteen more victories would come Little's way over the next three decades, en route to becoming the most winning Gold Cup owner in history.

The 1971 Gold Cup race is covered in Chapter Eight.

Delays, controversy and rough water marred the running of the 1974 Seattle Gold Cup, which was contested at Sand Point instead of the usual location, south of the Old Floating Bridge.

The on-shore difficulties not withstanding, the race still had much to offer the fans in terms of excitement. George

Henley in the "Winged Wonder" PAY 'n PAK and Howie Benns in the MISS BUDWEISER battled all day long in some of the finest competition ever witnessed in the long history of power boat racing. The outcome was in doubt, right down to the final checkered flag.

PAY 'n PAK ultimately prevailed and won the cup-- but only after a titanic struggle.

The 1976 Gold Cup at Detroit was won when Tom D'Eath held off a gutsy challenge from the Muncey-chauffeured ATLAS VAN LINES (former PAY 'n PAK) on extremely rough water in the winner-take-all Final Heat.

Designed by Ron Jones, Sr., MISS U.S. was the first Gold Cup winner with a cabover -- or forward-cockpit -- hull configuration.

A cabover can generally corner better and faster than its rear-cockpit, forward-engine-situated predecessor. Every Gold Cup winner since 1976 has steered from the front.

Following the death of eight-time Gold Cup winner Bill Muncey in the World Championship Race at Acapulco, Mexico, in 1981, Lee "Chip" Hanauer took over as driver for the ATLAS VAN LINES team, now owned by Bill's widow, Fran Muncey.

Hanauer and crew chief, Jim Harvey, pulled off a heart-stopping victory at Detroit in 1982. The new Rolls-Royce Merlin-powered ATLAS almost blew over during a Final Heat battle with defending champion, Dean Chenoweth, and the Rolls-Royce Griffon-powered MISS BUDWEISER. MISS BUDWIESER boasted far more horsepower than the ATLAS VAN LINES.

After trailing for the first few laps, Chip executed a daring maneuver and ducked inside of Dean. This forced the BUDWEISER to run a wider and longer track.

When the roostertails subsided, Hanauer and ATLAS had added a new chapter to American sports legend. This was the first of eleven Gold Cups won by Chip between 1982 and

1999. Bill would have been proud.

Over the years, quite a few boats have won three APBA Gold Cups. Several of these have even won three Gold Cups in succession, but not until 1987 did any boat ever win four Gold Cups. This amazing craft won in 1984 as ATLAS VAN LINES and in 1985-86-87 as MILLER AMERICAN. The ATLAS/MILLER was also the first Gold Cup winner to utilize turbine power.

Heading into the 1988 race at Evansville, Indiana, Chip Hanauer had an incredible win streak of six consecutive Gold Cups. For a few brief moments, that victory string appeared to be at an end. Hanauer's MILLER HIGH LIFE entry suffered hull damage in a collision with another boat and had to be withdrawn. Then Chip was offered the seat in the other Fran Muncey hydroplane, the MISS CIRCUS CIRCUS, which had been driven in the first two heats by John Prevost. Hanauer stepped in and won the last two heats, including the winner-take-all finale, to claim Gold Cup victory number seven since 1982.

Hometown Detroit driver, Mark Tate, made a vivid impression with a pair of Gold Cup triumphs in 1991 and 1994 for owner, Steve Woomer. In 1991, driving WINSTON EAGLE, Tate outran George Woods in EXECUTONE and Mike Hanson in VALVOLINE MISS MADISON. In 1994 with the same boat (renamed SMOKIN' JOE'S), Tate reeled off victories in all five Gold Cup heats.

Only two drivers in the modern era have managed to score back-to-back Gold Cup victories with two different teams. The first was Danny Foster, who won in 1947 with the Dossin brothers', MISS PEPS V and in 1948 with Albin Fallon's, MISS GREAT LAKES. The other was Dave Villwock, who tied down his first Gold Cup with PICO AMERICAN DREAM, owned by Fred Leland, in 1996 and his second with Bernie Little's, MISS BUDWEISER in 1997.

WINSTON EAGLE

Villwock has since claimed three additional Gold Cups for owner Little in 1998, 2000 and 2002. Dave's racing career almost ended following a serious accident in the 1997 Columbia Cup at the Tri-Cities, Washington.

MISS BUDWEISER "blew over" in the Final Heat and Villwock suffered the loss of two fingers on his right hand.

When the starting gun fired for the 1998 season-opener at Evansville, there was Dave Villwock, back in the MISS BUDWEISER cockpit, maintaining his familiar first-place.

One of the most popular Gold Cup wins in recent years was Mike Hanson's 2001 triumph with TUBBY'S GRILLED SUBMARINES, owned by Mike and Lori Jones.

The Jones boat had suffered major structural damage the week before at Madison, Indiana. So extensive was the damage that the team's appearance at the Gold Cup in Detroit seemed unlikely.

Instead of heading for home and missing the most important race of the year, driver Hanson, who is a boat builder by profession, sparked a round-the-clock repair effort. For several days, Mike and his crew hardly slept. When the starting gun fired at Detroit, the boat was ready to race. What a race it was.

Hanson and TUBBY'S GRILLED SUBMARINES exited the first turn of the Final Heat and pulled away to a decisive lead. The boat, which few had expected to even be there, was on its way to the bank. Greg Hopp and ZNETIX ran a distant second.

Mike Hanson wins the 2001 Gold Cup driving TUBBY'S GRILLED SUBMARINES.

The 2001 Gold Cup marked the first-ever victory in the Unlimited Class by the Jones Racing Team. Owner Mike Jones, who was president of the American Power Boat Association at the time, became the first sitting APBA President to win the APBA's Crown Jewel since Jonathon Wainwright in 1905.

The 2002 race at Detroit marked the fourteenth win by MISS BUDWEISER owner, Bernie Little, in the Gold Cup series and his fourth with driver, Villwock.

Little's previous pilots include Bill Sterett (1969). Dean Chenoweth (1970-73-80-81), Tom D'Eath (1989-90) and Chip Hanauer (1992-93-95).

Madison -- Hydroplane Heritage - Fred Farley & Ron Harsin

Gold Cup Winners

Year   Boat   Owner   Driver

2002 MISS BUDWEISER - Bernie Little - Dave Villwock
2001 TUBBY'S GRILLED SUBMARINES - Mike & Lori Jones - Mike Hanson
2000 MISS BUDWEISER - Bernie Little - Dave Villwock
1999 MISS PICO - Chip Hanauer
1998 MISS BUDWEISER - Bernie Little - Dave Villwock
1997 MISS BUDWEISER - Bernie Little - Dave Villwock
1996 PICO AMERICAN DREAM - Fred Leland - Dave Villwock
1995 MISS BUDWEISER - Bernie Little - Chip Hanauer
1994 SMOKIN' JOES - Steve Woomer - Mark Tate
1993 MISS BUDWEISER - Bernie Little - Chip Hanauer
1992 MISS BUDWEISER - Bernie Little - Chip Hanauer
1991 WINSTON EAGLE - Steve Woomer - Mark Tate
1990 MISS BUDWEISER - Bernie Little - Tom D'Eath
1989 MISS BUDWEISER - Bernie Little - Tom D'Eath
1988 CIRCUS CIRCUS - Fran Muncey - Chip Hanauer
1987 MILLER AMERICAN - Fran Muncey - Chip Hanauer
1986 MILLER AMERICAN - Fran Muncey - Chip Hanauer
1985 MILLER AMERICAN - Fran Muncey - Chip Hanauer
1984 ATLAS VAN LINES - Fran Muncey - Chip Hanauer
1983 ATLAS VAN LINES - Fran Muncey - Chip Hanauer
1982 ATLAS VAN LINES - Fran Muncey - Chip Hanauer
1981 MISS BUDWEISER - Bernie Little - Dean Chenoweth
1980 MISS BUDWEISER - Bernie Little - Dean Chenoweth
1979 ATLAS VAN LINES - Bill Muncey - Bill Muncey
1978 ATLAS VAN LINES - Bill Muncey - Bill Muncey
1977 ATLAS VAN LINES - Bill Muncey - Bill Muncey
1976 MISS U S - George Simon - Tom D'Eath
1975 PAY n' PAK - D. Heerensperger - George Henley
1974 PAY n' PAK - D. Heerensperger - George Henley

Madison -- Hydroplane Heritage - Fred Farley & Ron Harsin

1973 MISS BUDWEISER - Bernie Little - Dean Chenoweth
1972 ATLAS VAN LINES - Joe Schoenith - Bill Muncey
1971 MISS MADISON - City of Madison, Indiana - Jim McCormick
1970 MISS BUDWEISER - Bernie Little - Dean Chenoweth
1969 MISS BUDWEISER - Bernie Little - Bill Sterret
1968 MISS BARDAHL - Ole Bardahl - Bill Schumacher
1966 TAHOE MISS - Bill Harrah - Mira Slovak
1965 MISS BARDAHL - Ole Bardahl - Ron Musson
1964 MISS BARDAHL - Ole Bardahl - Ron Musson
1963 MISS BARDAHL - Ole Bardahl - Ron Musson
1962 MISS CENTURY 21 - Thriftway Stores - Bill Muncey
1961 MISS CENTURY 21 - Thriftway Stores - Bill Muncey
1960 - No Race
1959 MAVERICK - W. Waggoner, Jr. - Bill Stead
1958 HAWAII KAI III - Jack Regas
1957 MISS THRIFTWAY - Willard Rhodes - Bill Muncey
1956 MISS THRIFTWAY - Willard Rhodes - Bill Muncey
1955 GALE V - Joe Schoenith - Lee Schoenith
1954 SLO MO SHUN V - S. Sayres - Lou Fageol
1953 SLO MO SHUN IV - S. Sayres - Lou Fageol
1952 SLO MO SHUN IV - S. Sayres - Stan Dollar
1951 SLO MO SHUN V - S. Sayres - Lou Fageol
1950 SLO MO SHUN IV - S. Sayres - Ted Jones
1949 MY SWEETIE - Bill Cantrell
1948 MISS GREAT LAKES - A. Fallon - Dan Foster
1947 MISS PEPS V - The Dossins - Dan Foster
1946 TEMPO VI - Guy Lombardo - Guy Lombardo
1945 No Race
1944 No Race
1943 No Race
1942 No Race
1941 MY SIN - Zalmon Guy Simmons - Zalmon Guy Simmons
1940 HOTSY TOTSY III - Sidney Allen - Sidney Allen

1939 MY SIN - Zalmon Guy Simmons - Zalmon Guy Simmons
1938 ALAGI - Theo Rossi - Theo Rossi
1937 NOTRE DAME - Herb Mendelson - Clell Perry
1936 IMPSHI - Horace E. Dodge Jr. - Kaye Don
1935 EL LAGARTO - George C. Reis - George C. Reis
1934 EL LAGARTO - George C. Reis - George C. Reis
1933 EL LAGARTO - George C. Reis - George C. Reis
1932 DELPHINE IV - Horace E. Dodge - Bill Horn
1931 HOTSY TOTSY - Vic Kliesrath - Vic Kliesrath
1930 HOTSY TOTSY - Vic Kliesrath - Vic Kliesrath
1929 I M P III - Richard F. Hoyt - Richard F. Hoyt
1928 No Race
1927 GREENWICH FOLLEY - George H. Townsend - George H. Townsend
1926 GREENWICH FOLLEY - George H. Townsend - George H. Townsend
1925 BABY BOOTLEGGER - Caleb Bragg - Caleb Bragg
1924 BABY BOOTLEGGER - Caleb Bragg - Caleb Bragg
1923 PACKARD CHRISCRAFT - Jesse Vincent - Caleb Bragg
1922 PACKARD CHRISCRAFT - Jesse Vincent - Jesse Vincent
1921 MISS AMERICA - Gar Wood - Gar Wood
1920 MISS DETROIT IV - Gar Wood - Gar Wood
1919 MISS DETROIT III - Gar Wood - Gar Wood
1918 MISS DETROIT III - Gar Wood - Gar Wood
1917 MISS DETROIT II - Gar Wood - Gar Wood
1916 MISS MINNEAPOLIS - Miss Minneapolis Boat Assoc. Bernard Smith
1915 MISS DETROIT - John "Freckles" Milot
1914 BABY SPEED DEMON II - J. Stuart Blackton - R. Edgren
1913 ANKLE DEEP - Casimir Mankowski - Casimir Mankowski

Madison -- Hydroplane Heritage - Fred Farley & Ron Harsin

1912 PDQ II - A. Graham Miles - A. Graham Miles
1911 MIT II - J. H. Hayden - J. H. Hayden
1910 DIXIE III - F. K. Burnham - F. K. Burnham
1909 DIXIE II - E. J. Schroeder - Jonathan Wainwright
1908 DIXIE II - E. J. Schroeder - Jonathan Wainwright
1907 CHIP II - Jonathan Wainwright - Jonathan Wainwright
1906 CHIP II - Jonathan Wainwright - Jonathan Wainwright
1905 CHIP - Jonathan Wainwright - Jonathan Wainwright
1904 VINGT ET UN II - W. S. Kilmer - W. S. Kilmer
1904 STANDARD - C. C. Riote - Carl Riote
FIRST GOLD CUP - 1904

Madison -- Hydroplane Heritage - Fred Farley & Ron Harsin

Chapter Two
History Of Hydroplane Racing

Vintage Hydroplanes

The four major design changes are shown in the following photographs of these Gold Cup Winning hydroplanes.

MISS AMERICA I

Madison -- Hydroplane Heritage - Fred Farley & Ron Harsin

MISS PEPS V

SLO-MO-SHUN V

Madison -- Hydroplane Heritage - Fred Farley & Ron Harsin

Bill Muncey in the Gold Cup winning "Blue Blaster"
ATLAS VAN LINES

BABY GAR IV & V

The only known color photo in existence of the "BILL-DER" may be viewed in the color inset section of this book. Photo taken in Madison, Indiana.

33

Madison -- Hydroplane Heritage - Fred Farley & Ron Harsin

MISS DESOTO

Future MISS MADISON driver Buddy Byers won many races with the 7-Liter Class MISS DESOTO in the 1950's

The "NITROGEN" and the "NITROGEN TOO" running side by side. The NITROGEN would become the 1st MISS MADISON and the NITROGEN TOO would become the 2nd MISS MADISON.

Madison -- Hydroplane Heritage - Fred Farley & Ron Harsin

Limited Hydroplanes

For years, the Madison Regatta Association has offered spectators a series of Unlimited and Limited Hydroplane races. Over the years the racing has had different formats. At one time the Limited Hydroplanes raced on Saturday and the Unlimiteds on Sunday. On other occasions the Limited Hydroplanes raced between the Unlimited Hydroplane heats.

Madison has long been known for being the home of several Unlimited Hydroplanes, yet very few people realize how many Limited Hydroplanes come from Madison.

The following Limited Hydroplanes are now, or have been, based in Madison, Indiana.

GP-317 Valleyfield 99 BIG WAVE
Bill Fisk - Driver

MISS CLOSE SHAVE II
Dave Johnson - Owner/Driver

35

Madison -- Hydroplane Heritage - Fred Farley & Ron Harsin

RIDE-ON
Denny Jackson - Driver

HINKLE'S SANDWICH SHOP
Denny Jackson - Driver

Madison -- Hydroplane Heritage - Fred Farley & Ron Harsin

A popular entry on the Unlimited Light Racing Series tour in recent years has been the HINKLE'S SANDWICH SHOP entry and is sponsored by a popular Madison restaurant. HINKLE'S pilot, Denny Jackson, a veteran of the inboard hydroplane wars, won the fifth-place trophy at the 2000 Madison Regatta.

W D RACING
Wayne Dunlap - Owner/Driver

En route to victory in the 2.5 Litre Stock Class at the 2002 Madison Regatta

Madison -- Hydroplane Heritage - Fred Farley & Ron Harsin

OPC Tunnel Boat
Jeff Knox of Madison, IN has competed on the OPC Tunnel Boat Circuit for many years.

28H Outboard Hydroplane
Matt Sontag - Owner/Driver

Chapter Three
Gone But Not Forgotten

PART I

Black Sunday Unlimited Hydroplane Racing's Darkest Day

For most Americans, growing up in the middle of the 20th Century, two dates are burned indelibly into the collective consciousness. Those of the World War II generation, December 7, 1941, Pearl Harbor Day, was a defining moment. For the Baby Boomers, it was November 22, 1963, when an assassin's bullet took the life of President John F. Kennedy. Seemingly everyone old enough to remember can recall, with vivid detail, where they were and what they were doing at the exact moment that these tragedies occurred.

For post-war Unlimited hydroplane devotees, a third such date is remembered for all of its gut-wrenching intensity. It was June 19, 1966, "Black Sunday," when three of racing's finest were lost in two separate accidents at the President's Cup Regatta in Washington, D.C. Stricken from the list of the living on that fateful day were Ron Musson of MISS BARDAHL, Rex Manchester of NOTRE DAME and Don Wilson of MISS BUDWEISER.

Musson perished when his radically-designed craft, running in only its second heat of competition, became airborne and crashed to the bottom of the Potomac River, while battling for the lead in Heat 2-B. Manchester and Wilson were killed when their boats collided while contending for first-place in Heat Three.

The loss of Musson, Manchester and Wilson shook the boat racing world to its foundation. The impact would have been similar if Mario Andretti, A.J. Foyt and Dan Gurney had been lost in a single afternoon. Like their auto racing counterparts, Ron, Rex and Don were professional athletes, loved and admired by thousands of fans. They were role models for a generation of young racing fans.

People in the sport felt a special grief in the aftermath of Black Sunday. The late Bill Muncey once told an interviewer that, for the rest of his life, not a week would pass when he wouldn't think about his three fallen comrades.

Wilson had been Muncey's roommate in college and it was Bill who had recommended Musson be hired to drive for Ole Bardahl in 1961.

In truth, no one who experienced the 1966 President's Cup will ever forget it. June 19 was truly the sport's darkest day.

In its first two decades after World War II, Unlimited hydroplane racing saw six fatalities. Driver, Orth Mathiot and riding mechanic, Thom Whitaker were killed when QUICKSILVER crashed at Seattle in 1951. MISS SUPERTEST II pilot, Bob Hayward, perished at Detroit in 1961.

It was a cruel twist of fate when half of the sport's

casualties occurred within three hours of each other.

Unlimited, or Thunderboat, racing had grown out of the ashes of the pre-war Gold Cup and 725 Cubic Inch Classes. After World War II a huge supply of fighter plane engines became available to the general public.

The Packard Rolls-Royce Merlin, the G.M. Allison and the propriding three-point hull design, developed by Ted Jones, transformed the sport. By the mid-1950s, the Unlimiteds were the showcase of APBA racing. In 1957, the parent American Power Boat Association allowed the Unlimited Class to break away from the administrative restraints of the Inboard Racing Commission and form a separate APBA entity.

The early 1960's witnessed the dawn of professionalism with mandatory cash prizes at every Unlimited event. In 1963, the IRS upheld the Unlimited Racing Commission's contention that Thunderboating was a legitimate business expense, within specified guidelines and thereby, tax deductible. This opened the door to big money, corporate sponsorship on a scale previously unimagined.

One of the first companies to sponsor an Unlimited hydroplane on a large national scale was Anheuser-Busch, which introduced the MISS BUDWEISER, owned by Bernie Little, in 1964.

The 1965 racing season had been one of the more successful campaigns in history with 23 active boats and nine scheduled races. These included the APBA Gold Cup at Seattle and the UIM World Championship at Lake Tahoe, sanctioned by the Union of International Motorboating.

Musson and the MISS BARDAHL captured the Gold Cup (their third in as many years), the World Championship and the National High Points crown. Second in 1965 National Points was NOTRE DAME, driven by Manchester, who ironically, was Ole Bardahl's son-in-law. Rex won no races in 1965 but always gave the MISS BARDAHL a good battle.

At the last race of the year on San Diego's Mission Bay, Musson and the "Green Dragon" MISS BARDAHL became the first to turn a lap in competition at 117 miles per hour on a 3-mile course. The record provided an upbeat ending to the 1965 season, which had been highly competitive overall. The outlook for 1966 appeared bright indeed.

The first hint of the dark days to come occurred two months before the start of the season. URC official and former champion driver Bill Stead was fatally injured when his private plane went out of control while practicing an aerobatic maneuver and crashed into Tampa Bay.

Stead, a successful Nevada cattle rancher, had served as Unlimited Drivers' Representative since his retirement from competition in 1959. The man had class and his loss was keenly felt by the Thunderboat fraternity.

Nevertheless, the sport had a lot going for it at the outset of 1966. Some promising new race sites had been added to the Unlimited schedule; Tampa, Florida, Kelowna, British Columbia, the Tri-Cities, Washington, and Sacramento, California. The time-honored Washington, D.C., event was back on the calendar after a one-year hiatus.

The season-opening Tampa Suncoast Cup on June 12 attracted eighteen hopefuls. This was the largest first-day field for the Unlimiteds since 1949.

During the 1965-66 off season, host owner, Bernie Little, had acquired, the MISS EXIDE from Milo and Glen Stoen. Little had persuaded the EXIDE mechanical crew, headed by Bernie Van Cleave and George McKernan, to transfer en masse to the MISS BUDWEISER team, along with MISS EXIDE driver Bill Brow. This was the same group of competitive wizards who had won the 1965 Coeur d'Alene Diamond Cup so convincingly. They had also set the current world record of 120.536 for a 3-mile qualification lap at Seattle in 1965.

After three years of "also-ran" status in the Unlimited

ranks, Little now had an acknowledged front-runner. There could be no doubt that the "new" MISS BUDWEISER, a 1956 Ted Jones creation, would be a factor in the season ahead.

George Simon's MISS U.S. racing team had Bill Muncey, the all-time winningest Thunderboat pilot, at the wheel. Muncey had recently undergone successful surgery for a back ailment that had prevented him from accepting a full-time driving assignment in 1965. Bill had been on the fringes of the sport since being fired from NOTRE DAME in mid-season 1964. He was anxious to reaffirm his status as the sport's number one driver. Since the retirement of MISS THRIFTWAY in 1963, Muncey's career had not gone well.

Owner Simon had signed Bill to a five-year contract, starting with the last race of 1965. The MISS U.S. team had set a mile straight-a-way record of 200.419 in 1962 but hadn't won a race since 1958. Rex Manchester, Muncey's replacement in the NOTRE DAME cockpit, was in his seventh season as an Unlimited chauffeur, yet he had never won a race. This was a situation that Manchester vowed to rectify in 1966. NOTRE DAME, a 1964 Les Staudacher hull, was fast but had a tendency to ride roughly.

Owner, Shirley Mendelson McDonald, whose father (Herb Mendelson) had raced boats quite successfully between 1935 and 1947, had only one victory to her credit after four years in the sport. This was the 1964 Dixie Cup at Guntersville, Alabama, with Muncey driving.

Ron Musson was the defending National Champion and the sport's reigning superstar. Since his 1959 Unlimited Class debut, Musson had achieved winning results, almost from day one, with the HAWAII KAI III, NITROGEN TOO and MISS BARDAHL racing teams. His victory total of sixteen wins was second only to Muncey who, at the time, had nineteen first-place trophies.

Ron's 1966 chances were uncertain. Gone was the old reliable Green Dragon, designed by Ted Jones, that had served

Musson so well since 1962. The new MISS BARDAHL was a cabover creation from the drawing board of Ron Jones, Ted's son.

The 1966 BARDAHL was not the first Unlimited to seat the driver ahead of the engine. Other forward-cockpit boats included SANT' AMBROGIO and SKIP-A-LONG in 1948, SCOOTER in 1954 and THRIFTWAY TOO in 1957. MISS BARDAHL was patterned after a successful 225 Cubic Inch Class hydroplane, the TIGER TOO, built by Ron Jones in 1961. Unlike previous cabovers, TIGER TOO was wider and flatter and less box-shaped to allow for more effective cornering. The concept had yet to be proven in the Unlimited Class. There was a lot of prejudice against cabover hulls at the time as most people considered them unduly hazardous.

In the words of Bill Muncey, the driver of a forward-cockpit boat was "first to the scene of the accident," although even Muncey later changed his tune. Ron Musson, likewise, had some misgivings about cabovers, as did some members of the MISS BARDAHL mechanical crew. Musson obviously appreciated what Jones had done with TIGER TOO and was willing to give the new Green Dragon a try.

Musson was also grateful to Ron Jones for the excellent work he had done in fine-tuning the sponsons on the 1962 MISS BARDAHL. This work resulted in additional miles per hour for the boat.

Other new Unlimiteds at the 1966 Tampa race were Bill Sterett's, MISS CHRYSLER CREW and Jim Ranger's, MY GYPSY. The CHRYSLER CREW was the first serious attempt at twin-automotive power in the Thunderboats and was an enlarged hull duplicate (designed by Henry Lauterbach) of Sterett's 7-Litre Class, National Champion, MISS CRAZY THING. MY GYPSY was a typical Detroit riverboat from Gale Enterprises, designed by Bill Cantrell, in the tradition of the 1964 MISS SMIRNOFF and the 1965 GALE'S ROOSTERTAIL. Sponsored by the Dodge automotive family, Ranger took his rookie driver's test at Tampa with MY GYPSY and passed it, despite having had no previous experience in race boats.

Brow and MISS BUDWEISER qualified fastest at Tampa with a speed of 106.132; Musson and MISS BARDAHL were next at 103.806 on the 2 1/2 mile course. Tampa Bay was definitely one of the rougher venues in Unlimited history. The chop could be downright ocean-like at times. The fastest lap of the week was only 108.434, run by SMIRNOFF in Heat 2-C.

An early season hurricane ripped through southern Florida and inflicted major damage to the newly constructed pit area for the 1966 Suncoast Cup. The damage threatened cancellation of the race. In response, Bernie Little opened his checkbook and recruited every available laborer in Tampa to help clean up the debris so the race could be run as scheduled.

After three heats of racing, MISS U.S. and NOTRE DAME were tied with 1100 points apiece, based upon two firsts and one second-place finish. Manchester finished ahead of Muncey in the Final Heat of 15 miles, but MISS U.S. won the Suncoast Cup on the basis of a faster total elapsed time for the 45 miles. It was career win number twenty for Bill and another frustrating defeat for Rex.

In winning preliminary Heat 1-A over mediocre opposition, Manchester had backed off after the first three laps and cruised to the checkered flag at a leisurely 94.537 miles per hour. Muncey, on the other hand, had kept the pressure on and averaged 100.483 in Heat 1-B. Rex's laid-back performance in 1-A came back to haunt him at the end of the day and ultimately cost Manchester the race.

The Suncoast Cup emerged as something of a destruction derby. The victorious MISS U.S. suffered severe hull and sponson damage and had to cancel plans for the following weekend's President's Cup. The Chuck Thompson chauffeured SMIRNOFF, likewise, had to withdraw from the

Potomac River meet due to hull damage. Bill Brow took a bad bounce in Heat 1-C with MISS BUDWEISER, cracked his shoulder and had to be replaced by Don Wilson. The red-headed Wilson had last raced in 1964 as pilot of Simon's, MISS U.S. 5. Don had won the 1963 Lake Tahoe race as relief driver for Musson in the old MISS BARDAHL.

PART II

The anxiously awaited debut of the cabover MISS BARDAHL had to be put on hold at Tampa because a gearbox kept overheating, but the advance word on the new Green Dragon was favorable. According to crew chief LeoVanden Berg, the boat ran quite well in tests and could corner at over 100. This was at a time when most Unlimiteds could do 175 or more on the straightaway, but were unable to exceed 90 in the turns.

It was good news for designer Ron Jones. His fervent hope was for the 1966 MISS BARDAHL to be a trendsetter in the tradition of SLO-MO-SHUN IV, which his father had introduced so successfully in 1950.

Construction of the cabover BARDAHL had actually been completed the previous year. She would have raced in 1965 but for a delay in the arrival of component parts. The boat had experienced difficulty in spring testing. She carried too much weight in the rear and the crew had to shift weight forward to alleviate this problem. Now, at long last, MISS BARDAHL was ready to enter competition.

Heading into Washington, D.C., the odds-on favorite had to be NOTRE DAME. After being so close, so often, in the recent past, the Shamrock Lady was certainly overdue for a win. Owner, Shirley McDonald had fond feelings about the Potomac River race site. It was here where her father's boats had won in 1935, 1937 and 1940 with Clell Perry and Dan Arena as drivers. With two of the fleet's toughest competitors,

Madison -- Hydroplane Heritage - Fred Farley & Ron Harsin

MISS U.S. and SMIRNOFF, temporarily off the circuit, most observers confidently predicted that come Sunday, NOTRE DAME would take the President's Cup trophy home. So she did, but under well-known tragic circumstances.

Thirteen of the boats that appeared at Tampa made the trek to Washington. They were joined by the Detroit-based MISS DIXI COLA, handled by Fred Alter. Driving assignments from the previous week remained the same with Don Wilson continuing in his role as MISS BUDWEISER relief pilot. Wilson had won the 1958 President's Cup with MISS U.S. I.

Heats 1-A, 1-B and 1-C were run on Saturday, June 18. The first-place finishers were Sterett in MISS CHRYSLER CREW, Manchester in NOTRE DAME and Musson in MISS BARDAHL respectively. Twenty-four hours later, of the three Saturday winners, only Sterett remained alive. In notching Heat 1-A, the auto-powered MISS CHRYSLER CREW fooled the skeptics that predicted she wouldn't be competitive. Sterett outran Mira Slovak and TAHOE MISS, 99.337 to 99.228. Bob Fendler was a distant third with WAYFARERS CLUB LADY, followed by MY GYPSY, while Jim McCormick and MISS MADISON failed to finish.

Manchester and NOTRE DAME had the luck of the draw in Heat 1-B. Rex checked in first at an unhurried 96.826, the slowest winning speed of the weekend. The lesson of the previous Sunday on the matter of total elapsed time had apparently made no impression on Manchester. A distant-running Jerry Schoenith and GALE'S ROOSTERTAIL finished second, ahead of MISS DIXI COLA, while Walt Kade and SAVAIR'S MIST failed to finish.

The new MISS BARDAHL, running in competition for the first time, justified the faith of her owner, driver and designer. The Green Dragon dominated section 1-C and posted the fastest heat (101.218) and lap (102.975) of the entire race. The crew had feared that the 8000-pound craft would be hard on engines. This wasn't the case in Heat 1-C. MISS BARDAHL handled the Potomac River beautifully, an instant contender, just as TIGER TOO had been. The much-maligned cabover concept of Ron Jones all of a sudden had credibility.

Far behind the victorious Dragon, Wilson in MISS BUDWEISER and Warner Gardner in MISS LAPEER battled spectacularly for second place. Wilson took it, 95.238 to 95.026, while Norm Evans and $ BILL trailed in fourth. A crowd estimated at 40,000 turned out for the Sunday heats. Weather and water conditions were as close to perfect as possible. MISS MADISON had withdrawn, so the rest of the field was consolidated into two sections of six boats each for Heats 2-A and 2-B.

MISS BUDWEISER & MISS BARDAHL in competition before the fateful crashes.

Most people seemed upbeat after the successful series of Saturday heats, but Bob Carver, the dean of boat racing action photographers, felt strangely troubled. It was nothing that he could define. Something warned Carver that Sunday's racing would not go well, although Heat 2-A turned out to be brilliant.

Wilson and MISS BUDWEISER held off a formidable challenge from Sterett and MISS CHRYSLER CREW in one of the more aggressive contests in Thunderboat history. Sterett went all out after Wilson for four dynamic laps as the two powerhouses tore around the 2 1/2-mile oval. These were a couple of champion Mid-West Limited drivers, showing the fans what Unlimited racing is all about. BUDWEISER maintained first-place throughout, but CHRYSLER CREW was only a heartbeat behind.

A mechanical malfunction eventually halted Sterett's valiant drive for the lead. MISS CHRYSLER CREW then faded to sixth and last. Wilson knew that he'd been in a boat race. MISS BUDWEISER averaged 98.468 for the 15 miles. TAHOE MISS inherited second place at 95.759, followed by MISS LAPEER, $ BILL, MY GYPSY and MISS CHRYSLER CREW in that order.

The victory in Heat 2-A brought BUDWEISER's point total to 700, compared to 600 for TAHOE MISS. In order to surpass MISS BUDWEISER, both MISS BARDAHL and NOTRE DAME would have to win Heat 2-B.

Once again, it was Musson versus Manchester, the Mantle and Maris of boat racing, intense rivals out on the race course; close personal friends off it. Their families often fished and cruised together in the San Juans on their pleasure craft. Their wives, Betty Musson and Evelyn Bardahl Manchester, were also friends.

At the President's Cup in 1959, Ron Musson had qualified as an Unlimited driver, but despite many victories, the President's Cup was one award that had consistently eluded his grasp.

The crowd, which included Musson's teenage son Robert, tensed in anticipation as the field for Heat 2-B took to the water. The starting gun fired. MISS BARDAHL and NOTRE DAME exited the first turn together and charged down the backstretch. Once again, the cabover creation of Ron Jones was holding its own in the acid test of competition, as Musson raced full-tilt with NOTRE DAME.

The boats rounded the second turn, near National Airport and ran head-to-head down the front straight-a-way toward the completion of lap one. Then, according to Jones, the MISS BARDAHL's propeller sheared off and caused the prop shaft to twist into a corkscrew. The bow pitched skyward out of control. The Green Dragon slammed down hard and disintegrated, directly in front of the judges' stand.

The race announcer screamed, "It broke in two. The boat broke in two." MISS BARDAHL had, indeed, broken cleanly just behind the cockpit.

Rex Manchester, unaware of the accident, continued racing down into the next turn. Only when NOTRE DAME entered the backstretch did Rex see the red flare, signaling postponement. Musson was found floating face down. The boat that had debuted so promisingly the day before was a shattered wreck with the cockpit area completely destroyed. This was 1966; it was 1986 when the F-16 fighter plane safety canopy was introduced into Unlimited racing. The canopy likely could have saved Ron's life.

Musson, age 38, was pronounced dead on arrival at a local hospital. The man, widely regarded by hydroplane historians as the all-time greatest Unlimited driver, belonged to the ages. Not since Bob Hayward in 1961 had death visited Thunderboat racing. It was the first President's Cup fatality since Billy Frietag, driver of MISS PHILADELPHIA, a Gold Cup Class boat, in 1931.

Ron Jones blamed the propeller for the crash, although

MISS BARDAHL crew member Dixon Smith speculated that the boat may possibly have struck a log. Although everyone seemed to have a different opinion, there was no way to tell what had really happened. However, there could be no doubt of the end-result. The sport had lost its most prominent personality.

Ron Musson

MISS BARDAHL

Betty Musson learned of her husband's passing from Evelyn Manchester. Rex had called from Washington. Evelyn went over to the Musson home to console Betty. It was there, a few hours later, that Evelyn Manchester would learn of her own husband's death.

Back at the race site, the MISS BARDAHL pit crew picked up the pieces, while chief referee Bill Newton ordered a rerun of Heat 2-B. A distraught Jerry Schoenith would have no part of it and relinquished the seat in GALE'S ROOSTERTAIL to team manager Bill Cantrell.

The re-run of Heat 2-B was itself stopped. MISS DIXI COLA came to an abrupt halt while chasing NOTRE DAME and WAYFARERS CLUB LADY down the first backstretch. An overanxious course judge fired off a signal flare just as NOTRE DAME was about to finish lap one.

For the re-re-run, Cantrell persuaded Schoenith to reclaim the GALE'S ROOSTERTAIL cockpit. Jerry went out and finished third behind NOTRE DAME and SAVAIR'S MIST and ahead of WAYFARERS CLUB LADY. Manchester posted a winning speed of 97.192 with the rest of the field far astern.

This brought NOTRE DAME's point total to 800. Manchester led MISS BUDWEISER by 100 points going into the Final Heat. But Rex's lead in total elapsed time was only two seconds.

The NOTRE DAME team, then, had two options. They could finish first in the Final and win the race outright, or they could finish second to Don Wilson and tie the MISS BUDWEISER on points. The winner would then be determined on the basis of total elapsed time. NOTRE DAME would have to finish within two seconds of MISS BUDWEISER in order to claim the President's Cup.

For the second week in a row, Manchester's slow performance in Heat One had come back to haunt him.

Joining NOTRE DAME and MISS BUDWEISER in

the Final Heat were TAHOE MISS, GALE'S ROOSTERTAIL, MISS CHRYSLER CREW and MISS LAPEER. From the standpoint of speed, it was anybody's boat race. Of the six finalists, CHRYSLER CREW had the fastest competition lap of the weekend at 102.506, followed by BUDWEISER at 101.351, NOTRE DAME at 100.671, TAHOE MISS at 100.446, GALE'S ROOSTERTAIL at 96.983 and MISS LAPEER at 96.567.

A voice over the public address system at the five-minute gun confirmed what was already obvious -- Ron Musson had died. There were tears in Wilson's eyes as he steered MISS BUDWEISER away from the dock. In the 1950s, Musson and Wilson had raced Limiteds together on the Mid-West Inboard circuit. Don vowed to "win the race for Ron."

Manchester sat motionlessly in the NOTRE DAME cockpit. The five-minute gun fired and there was still no movement from Rex as the boat drifted aimlessly away from the dock. Finally, at the last possible moment, Manchester cranked the Rolls-Royce Merlin engine. NOTRE DAME roared to life and headed for the race course.

At the two previous Unlimited Class fatalities in the 1961 Silver Cup (Detroit) and the 1951 Gold Cup (Seattle), the races were cancelled and not resumed. The winners were determined on the basis of points scored in preliminary heats. The drivers at the 1966 President's Cup all voted to continue racing, a decision that would later be criticized.

The boats came around for the start of the Final Heat with MISS BUDWEISER in lane one and NOTRE DAME in lane two. MISS CHRYSLER CREW, TAHOE MISS and MISS LAPEER occupied lanes three, four and five respectively with GALE'S ROOSTERTAIL failing to start. Wilson and Manchester crossed the starting line together and stayed together through the first turn. MISS BUDWEISER thundered down the backstretch in first place with NOTRE

DAME close behind. Manchester found extra fire in the engine room and pulled along side Wilson as the two neared the National Airport turn.

MISS BUDWEISER was running rock steady, but NOTRE DAME was starting to get out of attitude. Manchester, nevertheless, kept going at top speed. MISS BUDWEISER backed off slightly to set up for the turn, but NOTRE DAME kept the power on in hopes of coming out of the turn first. NOTRE DAME became airborne, bounced on the left sponson, then on the right sponson and then hooked uncontrollably into lane one, just as MISS BUDWEISER reached the same spot.

A photographer from LIFE MAGAZINE captured the moment of impact: an explosion of water and boat pieces with the lifeless body of Don Wilson hurtling through the air. MISS BUDWEISER's bow had speared the underside of NOTRE DAME. When the spray subsided, nothing remained of the two boats. Both had already sunk to the bottom of the Potomac.

PART III

The other drivers swerved frantically to avoid the scene of the crash. Mira Slovak dove from the TAHOE MISS into the water and held Wilson's face out of the water until the arrival of a Coast Guard patrol craft. Nine years earlier, Slovak had likewise gone to the aid of Bill Muncey when MISS THRIFTWAY disintegrated at Madison, Indiana. Divers freed Manchester from the NOTRE DAME wreckage almost immediately.

Wilson, age 37, was already dead from a ruptured heart. Manchester, 39, had a broken neck and a nearly severed left leg. He lived for less than an hour and never regained consciousness.

Madison -- Hydroplane Heritage - Fred Farley & Ron Harsin

Don Wilson

MISS BUDWEISER

Rex Manchester

NOTRE DAME

The impact of this second tragedy -- occurring as it did so soon after the first -- hit everyone hard. According to HOT BOAT MAGAZINE writer Eileen Crimmin, the pit area became "a scene of mass shock, aimless wandering and thorough confusion."

This time, no attempt was made to reschedule the race. Referee Newton declared the 1966 President's Cup a contest on the basis of the preliminary action with NOTRE DAME announced as the winner.

For a while, Jim Hay, the crew chief of MISS CHRYSLER CREW, wouldn't take "No" for an answer. He demanded that the Final Heat be rerun. Hay and Bill Sterett almost came to blows but Sterett ultimately prevailed. "We're through for the day." Bill roared at Jim. "If they rerun the final, we won't be in it. Get that into your head."

Fred Alter demonstrated considerable class in the aftermath of Manchester and Wilson's crash. Alter went from one boat camp to another, bedding down the equipment, comforting the bereaved and being a tower of strength for those whose courage had failed.

A lot of angry words were spoken about the decision to continue after the Musson tragedy. "The race should have been stopped after the first accident," declared Warner Gardner. "None of us wanted to run after Ron's death," affirmed Bob Fendler. Bob Carver insisted that running the Final Heat was unnecessary, since all of the preliminary heats had been completed and the race could have legally been declared a contest.

MY GYPSY crew chief, Graham Heath, a close friend of Musson, had a difficult time, as did everyone else, in dealing with the loss. "I've been in racing where bad things occurred," Heath acknowledged. "But that was the worst blow to me that's ever happened. Afterwards, Graham did a lot of soul searching. "I thought to myself, 'We've got to be crazy. Sane people don't do this.' But there's just something about racing. It's in your blood."

Radio commentator Jim Hendrick refused to announce the fatality of Don Wilson, knowing that Wilson's elderly father was listening to the broadcast in Dearborn, Michigan. Hendrick did so over the violent objections of his producer, who wanted an "exclusive." That morning, Don had asked Jim to wish the older Wilson a happy Father's Day.

Past APBA President Red Peatross told THE NEW YORK TIMES, "The boats were well designed and constructed. The water was reasonably calm. Both accidents occurred on the straightaway, so the course layout can not be blamed. I guess all you can say is that it was an act of God."

Unlimited Commissioner J. Lee Schoenith predicted that the deaths would not have any great effect on the sport as a whole. All commitments with race sponsors would be honored, he promised. "But it sure isn't going to be the same type of season for the participants," Schoenith admitted. "These three gentlemen were my dearest and deepest friends."

Editorial reaction to the 1966 President's Cup ranged from sympathetic to extremely harsh.

In the words of THE SEATTLE TIMES writer Bud Livesley, "Three lives are a high price. Too high even for men, who for reasons known only to themselves, pursue speed and chase danger in boats."

Doc Greene of THE DETROIT NEWS proclaimed that "Death is the risk of those who defy it."

And Mel Crook, the respected YACHTING MAGAZINE columnist and a former Unlimited driver, pointed out that the safest boat in the world will eventually reach a speed where it travels unsafely. For a driver to place his boat in an unsafe attitude, even for the purpose of improving one's order of finish in a race, is to court disaster.

In response to the storm of criticism, Mira Slovak declared, "Sure, we're after speed. But we're not out to commit suicide. We're concerned with safety, too."

Madison -- Hydroplane Heritage - Fred Farley & Ron Harsin

Race Chairman Don Dunnington solemnly affirmed that there definitely would be a race in Washington, D.C. the following year. There was, but only for Limited boats. The Unlimiteds would not again race for the President's Cup until 1968.

On Capitol Hill, congressmen and senators expressed shock about the triple tragedy. President Lyndon B. Johnson called Washington Senator, Warren G. Magnuson, to express his concern. Magnuson said he was terribly shocked, especially since he had known Manchester and Musson personally.

Congressman Brock Adams, a Seattle Democrat, promised to look into the matter of how much control Congress had over races on the Potomac River. The race course, located in the District of Columbia, was governed by Congress. Improved standards were needed, Adams indicated.

In a letter of condolence from President Johnson to Evelyn Manchester, Johnson mentioned that Rex had been decorated for valor in the battle of Iwo Jima as a U.S. Marine in World War II. This was news to Evelyn. Rex, not a man to boast or to draw attention to himself, had never revealed this particular chapter in his life.

As a stunned and decimated Unlimited fraternity started packing to leave town, the realization dawned on some people that the winner of the ill-fated President's Cup was a guy named Rex Manchester. After a career of being "The best of the rest," Rex had finally achieved his ambition, albeit posthumously.

In the words of football legend Bear Bryant, the Unlimited participants "sucked up their guts" and went through the motions of business as usual two weeks later at Detroit, where another tragic day awaited the Thunderboats.

The newly repaired SMIRNOFF was back and stronger than ever. The race was for the Gold Cup, which driver, Chuck Thompson, had never won. Champion Chuck dominated Heats 1-B and 2-B and was clearly the class of the field. Thompson had come painfully close to capturing the 1952 and 1956 Gold Cups with MISS PEPSI and the 1964 race with TAHOE MISS. "This time I've got a winner," Chuck confided to his crew.

Thompson and SMIRNOFF were drawn into Heat 3-A, together with the combination of Slovak and TAHOE MISS, which had scored victories in Heats 1-A and 2-A.

The sport held its collective breath. Chuck was a give-no-quarter-and-ask-for-none kind of driver. Everyone knew that bad blood existed between Thompson and the TAHOE MISS organization, which had discharged Chuck at the end of the 1965 season.

Coming up for the start of Heat 3-A, Thompson and SMIRNOFF found their way blocked by Red Loomis and SAVAIR'S PROBE. Chuck had to decelerate momentarily but was back up to speed almost immediately. SMIRNOFF found an opening and shot forward with Thompson really standing on it.

Then as the field neared the Whittier Hotel in the run down to the Belle Isle Bridge turn, SMIRNOFF disappeared. According to Bill Newton, the boat seemed to become airborne momentarily and then smacked down hard on the water. SMIRNOFF disintegrated and sank immediately. The Allison engine was ripped completely out of the boat.

Chuck suffered a crushed chest, a fractured thigh and severe leg wounds. Thompson, age 54, passed away shortly after arrival at the hospital. He never regained consciousness. The death count had risen to four.

An Unlimited mainstay since 1949 and the winner of fifteen major races since 1950, Chuck had an intensely loyal fan following, especially in Detroit. He would be sorely missed.

Thompson's wife, Christine, witnessed the fatal crash. Their son, Chuck, Jr., was out of town that weekend, driving in a 280 Cubic Inch Class hydroplane race.

Initial response to the SMIRNOFF accident was panic. An official of the sponsoring Spirit Of Detroit Association went on local television to announce cancellation of the remaining Gold Cup heats. The race, he said, would be declared "No Contest." There were those who demanded the termination of the entire 1966 season. The sport's critics contended that Chuck Thompson had died for a brand name and that all forms of power boat competition, from outboards to Unlimiteds, should be abolished.

In time, cooler heads prevailed. APBA President Jim Jost stepped in and ordered that the Gold Cup be run to its conclusion, there being no provision in the APBA Gold Cup Rules for a "No Contest" result.

The race was completed on the following day, Monday, July 4. Slovak and TAHOE MISS took the honors.

Bill Cantrell, suffered burned hands at Tampa and had been replaced by Thompson in the SMIRNOFF cockpit. He spoke movingly and forcefully, "We're now at a pinnacle where the sport is going to go under or up." Cantrell reminded his comrades that Unlimited racing, together with Indianapolis racing, was a professional endeavor and professionals needed to act accordingly.

The Unlimited people took Cantrell's words to heart. The 1966 season went on as scheduled with a full field of participating boats. The level of competition was respectably high and compared favorably to 1965.

Doc Greene pointed out that "Abolition of the sport would not bring back Thompson and the others, nor their courage, nor their character; but would rather render meaningless, the sport for which they died."

All four of the new race sites in 1966 were declared successful and all four returned in 1967. Washington, D.C. and Coeur d'Alene, Idaho, did drop off the 1967 calendar but returned in 1968.

PART IV

TAHOE MISS won four races (Detroit, Kelowna, Coeur d'Alene and Madison) in 1966 and was National High Point Champion.

MISS BUDWEISER owner, Bernie Little, bought a previously unraced hull from builder Les Staudacher and was ready to go racing again only two weeks after Black Sunday. With Bill Brow at the wheel, Little scored his first-ever career win, the Tri-Cities Atomic Cup on July 24, followed by a triumph in the San Diego Cup on September 25.

Before season's end, MY GYPSY and MISS LAPEER likewise achieved victory at Seattle and Sacramento respectively.

When Evelyn Manchester, dressed in black, made an unexpected appearance at the Seattle Seafair Regatta drivers' meeting, she received enthusiastic applause and was invited by Cantrell to sit with the drivers.

The NOTRE DAME and the MISS BARDAHL teams did not re-appear in 1966. Both returned, however, in 1967 with new equipment. Owner, Ole Bardahl, abandoned the cabover concept and returned to a traditional rear cockpit-forward engine hull configuration.

Joe and Lee Schoenith continued on the 1966 tour with the former GALE'S ROOSTERTAIL hull renamed SMIRNOFF. Their best finish was a second place in the Atomic Cup with Cantrell driving.

The MISS U.S. team threw in the towel after Detroit. The boat suffered extensive damage when it fell into a hole during Heat 1-A of the Gold Cup and was declared unfixable. A new MISS U.S. was ordered for 1967 from Staudacher. In the interim, driver Muncey, filled in at three 1966 races as relief pilot of $ BILL.

The speeds attained in 1966 were admittedly down

Madison -- Hydroplane Heritage - Fred Farley & Ron Harsin

from 1965, but this was due, at least in part, to the large-scale transition from the 3-mile to the 2-1/2 mile race course. Although a few 3 mile courses still remained, the preferred course size was now 2-1/2 miles in the interest of improving spectator vantage points. With less distance to accelerate, the boats ran about 5 miles per hour slower lap speeds on a 2-1/2 mile track.

Despite the trauma of Black Sunday, the ensuing years of 1966 through 1975 provided a decade of racing unparalleled in Unlimited history. No apology need be made for the overall quality of competition during those ten pinnacle years. The racing was simply superb.

The sport did experience some additional down days during the 1966-1975 decade. Bill Brow was lost in 1967, Warner Gardner in 1968, Tommy Fults in 1970 and Skipp Walther in 1974.

The many great competitive duels that kept fans enthralled from coast-to-coast were downright legendary and on a par with many of the great races of the past. This was Unlimited Hydroplane racing at its best.

Not until the late 1970s did the sport go into a temporary decline due to the dwindling supply of World War II fighter aircraft engines. The turbine revolution of the 1980s restored the Unlimiteds to prominence, even if it meant taking the thunder out of the Thunderboats.

One long range effect of Black Sunday was re-enforcement of prejudice against cabover hulls in the Unlimited Class. Ron Jones kept insisting that the accident that took Ron Musson's life had nothing to do with the fact that the boat was a cabover, but it was associated with a cabover. And that made the concept difficult to sell for many years to come.

Jones produced an outstanding, 7-Litre Class cabover, the RECORD-7, owned by George Babcock, in 1969. RECORD-7 became the first Limited hydroplane to clear 100 miles per hour in a heat of competition. Even this was insufficient incentive for the Unlimited owners, as a whole, to invest in forward-cockpit hulls.

Owner Dave Heerensperger did try a Jones' cabover, the PRIDE OF PAY 'n PAK, in 1970. Heerensperger quickly gave up on the idea and converted his boat to a rear-cockpit configuration for 1971.

Not until 1977, when Bill Muncey introduced the ATLAS VAN LINES "Blue Blaster," designed by Jim Lucero and Dixon Smith, did the cabover concept gain wide acceptance in the Unlimited ranks.

In the decades following Black Sunday, the 1966 President's Cup has regrettably come to be regarded by some as the bad seed of Thunderboat racing. Deemed the cornerstone for everything, real or imagined, that is wrong with the sport.

A generation of editorial writers, many of whom never knew Musson, Manchester or Wilson, chose June 19, 1966, as the day when Unlimited hydroplane racing lost its innocence.

Hardly a year goes by without some enterprising journalist somewhere "discovering" the 1966 President's Cup. He or she will resurrect, with great relish, the ghosts of Ron, Rex and Don for yet another superficial "expose" to sell newspapers.

Not all of the after-effects of the 1966 President's Cup were negative. The Unlimited rules were significantly upgraded in the years that followed with a particular emphasis on safety. New requirements were written into the rulebook for adequacy of equipment. In the words of former URC Executive Secretary, Phil Cole, as published in the 1966-67 Unlimited Yearbook, "There emerged a better understanding of what can and must be done by the fleet that survived the rigors of 1966 to build a better sport for the future."

Looking at Black Sunday with a 21st Century perspective, a modern audience might be critical of a sport that

Madison -- Hydroplane Heritage - Fred Farley & Ron Harsin

was slow to embrace the concept of an enclosed cockpit.

As Dixon Smith stated in a 1996 interview with David Williams, the idea of seating a driver indoors was quite foreign at the time. If such a radical measure had been put to a vote in 1966, it likely would have been voted down. The belief was that in the event of an accident, the driver had a better chance for survival if he were thrown clear of his boat. For this reason, seat belts were prohibited in the Unlimited hydroplanes for many years.

Obviously, the boats in which Musson, Manchester, Wilson and Thompson died would not be allowed on the race course today but they were state of the art for their day.

For as long as men race boats, people will continue to speak in whispers about Black Sunday. It was a day too terrible to forget but there is some consolation in knowing that Ron, Rex, Don and Chuck died doing what they loved best.

The 1966 Sacramento Cup official program book was dedicated to the memory of Musson, Manchester, Wilson, Thompson and also Bill Stead. Editor Phil Cole chose a passage by Jack London as a fitting memorial to those five remarkable men:

"I would rather be ashes than dust."
"I would rather that my spark should burn out a brilliant blaze than it should be stifled by dryrot."
"I would rather be a superb meteor, every atom of me in magnificent glow, than a sleepy permanent planet."
"The proper function of man is to live, not to exist. I shall not waste my days by trying to prolong them. I shall use my time."

A Personal Memoir By Fred Farley
(APBA/HYDRO-PROP Unlimited Historian)

As Unlimited Historian, I've been asked many times how the tragic outcome of the 1966 President's Cup affected me as a hydroplane fan.

I remember "Black Sunday" as if it were yesterday. I was at home pounding away on my typewriter, writing copy for the 1966 Seafair Program, when I heard the news on the radio of Musson's death. It was a heart-sickening blow. After a while, I sat down and resumed typing. Then, when the Manchester/Wilson fatality was announced, I quit for the day.

The initial report on the second accident was simply "Two more fatalities in President's Cup," but the NBC radio network announcer didn't have the names.

My initial reaction was, "Oh great. Just our luck, it will be the other two Seattle-based boats (NOTRE DAME and MISS BUDWEISER)."

When the network switched back to the local station a few minutes later, the KING announcer had the names: Rex Manchester and Don Wilson. My premonition was so accurate it was unnerving.

Two days later, I attended the regularly scheduled meeting of the Seafair Regatta Committee at the Seattle Yacht Club. At that point, we didn't know if our race was going to be run. Everything was up in the air. The race chairman, Randy Pillow, went through the motions of business as usual, but everyone was devastated.

My good friend Bob Carver, the photographer, was there. He had just returned from Washington, D.C. I've never seen anyone look as "down" as Bob did at that meeting. He had been a close friend of Musson and Manchester.

As it turned out, Carver also had a premonition. On

Sunday, he had refused to go out in the photo boat, saying, "I don't take pictures of dead men."

This happened to be the committee meeting where the annual group photo was taken and this was the picture that appeared in the program. It shows all of us smiling, but that was the only time anyone smiled that day.

However, there was never any question that I would continue as a fan.

A lot of people walked away from the sport after "Black Sunday" and never returned. There comes a time in the life of every race fan when something happens and the person is confronted by an ugly reality. From then on, one can no longer look at the sport through rose-colored glasses.

For many fans, their particular "Waterloo" was the 1966 President's Cup. For me, it was the 1959 Diamond Cup at Coeur d'Alene. No one died at that race, seven years earlier, but there was a lot of carnage.

Jack Regas was critically injured in MISS BARDAHL.

Bill Brow was hurt and the MISS BURIEN was destroyed.

Chuck Hickling was likewise injured driving MISS PAY 'n SAVE.

Norm Evans was thrown out of MISS SPOKANE and suffered cuts.

That same weekend, Bob Doros, a Limited driver, was run over by another boat and lost an arm while racing the 280 Class WEE WAHOO for Mira Slovak at the Pasco Water Follies.

Slovak didn't have an Unlimited ride at Coeur d'Alene and was attending the Diamond Cup as a spectator. But when Hickling was hurt on Saturday, Mira was asked to take over the PAY 'n SAVE on Sunday. So Slovak arranged for Doros to drive the WEE WAHOO at Pasco.

In all, a grisly weekend of power boat racing.

Over the next few days, while Regas hovered between

life and death, I did a lot of soul searching. Quite frankly, I was at a crossroads. I had to decide: "Do I continue as a hydroplane fan, or do I cash in my emotional investment and walk away?" I nearly walked away.

Then, as Seafair time neared, I found myself getting caught up in the excitement of Gold Cup week. By race day, August 9, I was as "up" for the race as I had ever been and four decades later, I'm still at it. But, deep down, after the 1959 Diamond Cup, the sport was never quite the same.

That Coeur d'Alene race represented a "coming of age" on my part. From then on, I looked at racing with an adult's--not a child's--perspective. I had to accept the good breaks with the bad as part of life.

Part V

The Loss of Bill, Dean and Bernie

Bill Muncey Remembered

William Edward Muncey was an obscure, 225 Cubic Inch Class driver in the Mid-West during the late 1940s.

In 1950 he had a chance to drive Albin Fallon's MISS GREAT LAKES in the Harmsworth trials on the Detroit River. He was trying out for one of three spots on the U.S. Defense Team. The 21-year-old Muncey failed to make the final cut but he was able to pull an incredible 97 miles per hour out of the obsolete, MISS GREAT LAKES on a 5-nautical mile course. This was nothing short of amazing.

Bill reportedly had to be coached on the fine points of starting the huge Allison engine. Once out on the race course, there could be no doubt that a major new talent had arrived on the Unlimited scene.

Bill Muncey and The "Blue Blaster" ATLAS VAN LINES

Ted Jones was attending the same race with the SLO-MO-SHUN IV team. He was impressed by Muncey's performance in the MISS GREAT LAKES. A few year's later, when Jones was putting the MISS THRIFTWAY team together for Willard Rhodes, Ted remembered Bill and offered him the driver's job.

Muncey, by the way, also handled MISS GREAT LAKES in the 1950 Silver Cup but sank in the first heat. Bill likewise sank Horace Dodge, Jr.'s, DORA MY SWEETIE, at St. Clair, Michigan, in 1955. He then made the big time with MISS THRIFTWAY…and the rest is history.

Bill had a very erratic career. Not until 1960 did he ever win three heats in one day. Of course, any assessment of a driver's career has to take into account the quality of his competition.

Many of the top drivers of the 1950s were not a factor in the 1960s. Danny Foster, Bill Stead and Lee Schoenith had all retired. Jack Regas was retired for the time being and Bill Cantrell was stuck with a boat that wasn't very competitive.

In the 1950s, Muncey always seemed to have his act together at the Gold Cup, which he won in 1956 and 1957 and finished second in 1955 and 1959. His Gold Cups aside, Bill's record was very mediocre. In fact, Muncey only won two non-Gold Cup races during the entire decade of the '50s.

He had some great years in the early 1960s with the MISS THRIFTWAY (also known as MISS CENTURY 21). But some of those late 1960s seasons with the MISS U.S. were almost too pathetic to record.

It is a testament to the man's character that he was able to rebound from those "off" years and get his career back on track. After all, many a driver in many a class has ridden the crest of the victory wave when a well-financed boat was available. Rebounding from a career low spot is another matter entirely and that's exactly what Bill did in 1969.

There were those who wondered if Muncey still had what it took to be a winner in 1969. He was coming off two disastrous seasons. He was saddled with a boat that had an alarming tendency to fall on its nose at high speeds. His first wife had divorced him and he knew that his contract with MISS U.S. owner, George Simon, was not going to be renewed.

Yet, 1969 turned out to be one of his more exemplary years. He won a bona-fide victory at Detroit. He was competitive with the other top boats -- MISS BUDWEISER, MISS BARDAHL, NOTRE DAME and MYR'S SPECIAL -- and he stayed in the National High Points chase until the last day of the season.

It was in 1969 that Bill Muncey re-affirmed his greatness. Despite his flaws, Muncey deserves a favorable comparison with Gar Wood. Remember that Wood likewise had some "down" times during the middle 1920s.

Bill's longevity in the sport is also remarkable. How many drivers winning races in 1956 were still winning in 1981? Only Muncey.

He became his own owner in 1976, after a quarter century of driving for others. In partnership with crew chief Jim Lucero, Bill went on to achieve another Muncey golden age. He won 24 out of 34 races between 1976 and 1979 under the sponsorship of ATLAS VAN LINES.

Bill finally reached the end of the Thunderboat trail at Acapulco, Mexico, in 1981. By this time, he had won an unprecedented 62 victories in the Unlimited Class, including eight Gold Cups. While maintaining his familiar first-place, Muncey died in a "blow-over" accident during the Final Heat of the World Championship Race on Laguna de Coyucca.

Dean Chenoweth Remembered

Dean Chenoweth drove Unlimited hydroplanes from 1968 until his death in 1982. Like few drivers before or since, Dean could guarantee results. In so doing, he raised boat driving to art form.

Known primarily for his championship exploits with Bernie Little's MISS BUDWEISER team, Chenoweth won 25 Unlimited races. He captured the Crown Jewel of APBA competition, the Gold Cup, four times in 1970, 1973, 1980 and 1981. He also won four National High Point Championships and, in 1980, set a world lap speed record of 138.249 miles per hour on the Columbia River at the Tri-Cities, Washington.

Dean established a record of 20 consecutive heat victories at the first five races of 1980, driving the famed Rolls-Royce Griffon-powered MISS BUDWEISER.

Dean Chenoweth

Chenoweth won two races and finished second in National High Points in 1969 with Joe Schoenith's MYR'S SPECIAL, but felt that he could have, and should have, finished first. When Dean handed in his resignation at the end of 1969, he had not yet been offered the MISS BUDWEISER ride.

Chenoweth had one of his best seasons in 1973. His chief rival was PAY 'n PAK, piloted by Mickey Remund. Dean's boat was three years older and a thousand pounds heavier than PAY 'n PAK, but Chenoweth was, nevertheless, able to achieve parity with the PAK. This was due to Dean consistently securing the inside lane in heat confrontations between the two boats.

Beyond doubt, Dean Chenoweth's finest hour as a race

driver occurred on a cold, rainy, misty day on Seattle's Lake Washington in 1973. Visibility was terrible but water conditions were ideal. During the first heat of the World Championship, MISS BUDWEISER and PAY 'n PAK shared the same roostertail for five laps on a 3-mile course to become the first boats to average better than 120 miles per hour in a heat of competition.

MISS BUDWEISER

MISS BUDWEISER did 122.504, while PAY 'n PAK checked in at 120.697. The raw power and the competitive finesse of the two boats were positively awesome. This was what hydroplane racing was all about.

Despite being retired from the sport between 1974 and 1979, Chenoweth proved himself to be as competitive as ever in his later years.

Even in the last year of his life, Dean was nothing short of sensational. At season's end in 1981, Chenoweth had won six of eight races, including the Gold Cup in Seattle and the World Cup in Acapulco, Mexico.

Between 1980 and 1982, Chenoweth won more races than any other Unlimited driver and was Gold Cup and High Points Champion in 1980 and 1981.

Dean was leading in National Points when he suffered fatal injuries in a "blow-over" accident at the Tri-Cities in 1982.

Bernie Little Remembered

Bernie Little, the most successful owner in the history of Unlimited hydroplane racing, passed away on April 25, 2003, after a battle with pneumonia. A resident of Lakeland, Florida, he was 77.

In 2002, he celebrated his 40th year in racing and won his 22nd World High Points Championship with the MISS BUDWEISER, sponsored by Anheuser-Busch.

Between 1963 and 2002, Little's boats participated in 354 Unlimited races. His team finished in the top three a total of 230 times with a record 134 victories.

It all started when August A. Busch III recognized America's growing interest in water-oriented sports activities. With typical Busch shrewdness, he looked around for an attractive, colorful showcase to project the Budweiser image to growing millions of pleasure boaters.

Mr. Busch discussed the opportunity with his friend Bernie Little and it was decided to enter the glamorous and competitive world of Unlimited hydroplane racing. Thus was born the MISS BUDWEISER, a fixture on the Thunderboat circuit for the next four decades.

Before the very first "Beer Wagon" appeared on the Unlimited scene, many boats have vied for success. Some were unbeatable, some were mediocre and some crashed in splinters. But the quest has always been the same: to have a boat that represents the excellence of its corporate sponsor in a manner that reflects credit and prestige on the sport in which it is involved.

Although the first craft to carry the Anheuser-Busch "Eagle" into competition wasn't the fastest boat on the circuit, it became a publicity bonanza. Owner Little thoughtfully equipped the boat with four seats instead of the usual one or two. That turned the craft into a magnet around the Unlimited circuit.

Astronauts, politicians, television stars and journalists were waiting in line for a chance to "go for a ride" at 150 miles per hour. Newspaper reporters and broadcasters couldn't wait to get back to their typewriters, microphones and cameras after the thrilling trip.

The four-seater was an instant and continuing media hit but she lacked fire in the engine room. Providing four seats meant providing extra strength and extra weight to support it. That slowed her down.

Having won the publicity championship, August Busch and Bernie Little went searching for bigger game and made a full commitment to the sport. They won their first race in 1966 and their first Gold Cup and High Points Championship in 1969. MISS BUDWEISER went on to represent the longest continuous sponsorship in motor sports history.

Bernard Leroy Little was not born to great wealth. A native of McComb, Ohio, Little's upbringing partly reflected the Great Depression, which affected so many of his generation. His father's grocery store was a casualty of the economic instability of the times. Money was scarce.

"I went to work at an early age, " Little remembered. "I peddled newspapers, shoveled snow, carried golf bags over my back, whatever it took to get the job done. I've been working 12, 14, 16 hours a day ever since. That's the only life I know."

Bernie Little

Circumstances intervened to prevent Little from going past the eighth grade in school. He nonetheless had a high regard for the value of formal schooling in contemporary society. "The advice I would give young people today is education, education, education. That's the most important ingredient for a modern-day success story. You can't do today what I did a long time ago."

Madison -- *Hydroplane Heritage* - *Fred Farley & Ron Harsin*

At the age of 17, he joined the U.S. Navy and served during World War II. On an April night in 1945, Bernie, now a bosun's mate, found himself aboard the USS MARATHON, a troop ship moored off Okinawa. Without warning, a Japanese suicide submarine crashed into the vessel's hull and the MARATHON was on fire. Little was one of 36 survivors.

"Man, when you scramble out onto a burning ship's deck, jump into the water, into smoke, oil and flames in the middle of the night, that's fear," he remembered. "That's the scaredest 'Little' Bernie's ever been."

After returning to civilian life, Little established the foundation for a business dynasty in aircraft and transportation sales. He and his wife, Jane, settled in Florida in the 1950s with their children, Bernie, Jr., Joe and Becky.

Little's passion for flying led to a career as a stunt pilot with the All-Miami Air Show and later as a pioneer in Florida's helicopter sales industry. Since an Unlimited hydroplane really has more in common with an airplane than a boat, it was only natural that Little would gravitate to the greatest show in water racing.

Bernie's long association with the MISS BUDWEISER reflected his genius for marketing and sales promotion. This same expertise accounted for the tremendous success of his three Anheuser-Busch distributorships in Florida.

"I like speed and competition, " Little admitted. "I like a good challenge. And I just want to be better, faster and safer than anyone else on the race course."

Despite his many victories and record performances with the MISS BUDWEISER, Little always considered his greatest triumph to be the development of the enclosed cockpit. When Little's driver and close friend Dean Chenoweth was tragically lost in a "blow-over" accident at the Tri-Cities (Washington) Columbia Cup in 1982, Little realized that something had to be done to make the sport "safer and safer, not just faster and faster."

In 1985, Little and crew chief Jeff Neff introduced the famed "Bubble" BUD, the first Unlimited hydroplane to seat the driver, Jim Kropfeld, "indoors." The following year, designer Ron Jones, Sr., installed the first F-16 fighter plane canopy on another MISS BUDWEISER.

The Unlimited Racing Commission was quick to recognize the viability of the F-16 canopy. Starting in 1987, all new boats in the Unlimited Class were required to have them. The older ones were given until 1989 to make the change-over.

Thanks to the F-16 canopy, many drivers have literally walked away from accidents that previously would have been fatal.

If not for the canopy, MISS BUDWEISER pilot Dave Villwock would likely not have survived his horrific crash on the Columbia River at the 1997 Tri-Cities race.

"Safety has always been first in my mind," Little said. "I'm not a very good loser but I don't believe in winning at any cost, especially when it is a matter of a driver's life.

"I wouldn't want my driver out there on the race course without giving him every bit of protection that is available."

All of his accomplishments in racing and business not withstanding, Little was a deeply committed family man. The center of his private world was Jane, whom he courted and married in nine days in 1944, and their three children and four grandchildren.

According to Bernie, his Unlimited hydroplane career was very much a family endeavor. "Without Jane, I never would have stayed with it for as long as I have, because it took so much dedication on her part to make it all come true."

Little also prized his relationship to the Busch family, which remained strong over the years. In fact, Bernie introduced August Busch III to Ginny, the woman who would become Busch's wife.

"I was one of the best men at the wedding," said Little.

"Their children are like my grandchildren. We are just a very close family, always together."

After 40 years in the sport, Bernie had a long list of special MISS BUDWEISER "moments." These included his first-ever victory as an Unlimited owner at the Tri-Cities in 1966 with driver Bill Brow and his first APBA Gold Cup victory at San Diego in 1969 with pilot Bill Sterett.

Then there was that memorable day at Seattle in 1973 when MISS BUDWEISER, in a driving rain, became the first to average over 120 miles per hour in a heat of competition with Dean Chenoweth at the wheel.

Who could ever forget that incredible string of 20 consecutive heat victories by Chenoweth at the first five races of the 1980 season.

Little also noted with pride the many heroic repair jobs performed over the years by the MISS BUDWEISER mechanical crew. That includes the time at the 1988 Columbia Cup when the boat sustained major damage during a test run on Friday of race week. A lot of work needed to be done in a hurry at the team's Seattle shop, 220 miles away.

By Sunday morning, crew chief Ron Brown had MISS BUDWEISER repaired and ready. The "Beer Wagon" and driver Tom D'Eath went on to score another victory for Anheuser-Busch.

"Slap an order like that on most teams and you'd have chaos," Little pointed out. "But when you've got a crew like the MISS BUDWEISER, anything's possible. They have more survival instincts than a commando squad under fire."

Like every other American, Bernie Little was shaken to the core by the terrorist attacks of September 11, 2001. Solemn but undaunted, the MISS BUDWEISER team went ahead with business as usual at the race in San Diego a few days later. It was on San Diego's Mission Bay where BUDWEISER driver Villwock clinched the team's 21st World Championship.

"My reaction to the terrorist attacks was that we had to go ahead and race to prove that no one can stop what's going on in the United States. We just couldn't let that disaster stop the whole world. So, in our own way, we proved that life could go on. We're too big, too strong and there are too many of us to let tragedies bring us to a standstill. It was the right decision to keep moving forward."

Bernie approached his 40th, and last, season of Unlimited hydroplane competition with the same dedication as the first 39. At the outset of 2002, Little set three goals for his team: a victory in the opening-day race at Evansville, Indiana; a 14th Gold Cup at Detroit; and a 22nd World High Points Championship. MISS BUDWEISER succeeded on all three counts with driver Villwock and crew chief Mark Smith.

Bernie's 134th and final race victory, occurred at the 2002 General Motors Cup on Seattle's Lake Washington, where MISS BUDWEISER finished first in all four heats. "I'll have a smile all the way home," proclaimed a jubilant Little.

Widely known as "The King of Boats," Bernard Leroy Little was a virtual personification of the corporate slogan, "Making Friends Is Our Business." His broad smile, handshake and resonant greeting were almost as familiar as the trademarked "A & Eagle" logo.

In his life and hydroplane career, Bernie represented the qualities of aggressiveness, hard work and ingenuity that have led many Americans to achieve greatness.

Salute and farewell, Bernie Little.

Madison -- Hydroplane Heritage - Fred Farley & Ron Harsin

MISS BUDWEISER RACE VICTORIES (1966-2002)

Year   City   Driver   Crew Chief

(1) 1966 - Tri-Cities, WA - Bill Brow - George McKernan
(2) 1966 - San Diego, CA - Bill Brow - George McKernan
(3) 1967 - Kelowna, BC - Mike Thomas - George McKernan
(4) 1968 - Phoenix, AZ - Bill Sterett - George McKernan
(5) 1969 - Guntersville, AL - Bill Sterett - George McKernan
(6) 1969 - Owensboro, KY - Bill Sterett - George McKernan
(7) 1969 - Seattle, WA - Bill Sterett - George McKernan
(8) 1969 - San Diego, CA - Bill Sterett - George McKernan (GOLD CUP)
(9) 1970 - Tampa, FL - Dean Chenoweth - George McKernan
(10) 1970 - Madison, IN - Dean Chenoweth - George McKernan
(11) 1970 - Seattle, WA - Dean Chenoweth - George McKernan
(12) 1970 - San Diego, CA - Dean Chenoweth - George McKernan (GOLD CUP)
(13) 1971 - Miami, FL - Dean Chenoweth - George McKernan
(14) 1971 - Detroit, MI - Dean Chenoweth - George McKernan
(15) 1973 - Owensboro, KY - Dean Chenoweth - Tom Frankhouser
(16) 1973 - Detroit, MI (June) - Dean Chenoweth - Tom Frankhouser
(17) 1973 - Tri-Cities, WA - Dean Chenoweth - Tom Frankhouser (GOLD CUP)
(18) 1973 - Detroit, MI (Sept) - Dean Chenoweth - Tom Frankhouser
(19) 1974 - Miami, FL - Howie Benns - Tom Frankhouser
(20) 1974 - Detroit, MI - Howie Benns - Tom Frankhouser

Madison -- Hydroplane Heritage - Fred Farley & Ron Harsin

(21) 1974 - Phoenix, AZ - Howie Benns - Tom Frankhouser
(22) 1974 - Jacksonville, FL - Dean Chenoweth - Tom Frankhouser
(23) 1975 - Washington, DC - Mickey Remund - Tom Frankhouser
(24) 1975 - Phoenix, AZ - Mickey Remund - Tom Frankhouser
(25) 1976 - Seattle, WA - Mickey Remund - Tom Frankhouser
(26) 1977 - Madison, IN - Mickey Remund - Tom Frankhouser
(27) 1977 - Dayton, OH - Mickey Remund - Tom Frankhouser
(28) 1977 - San Diego, CA - Mickey Remund - Tom Frankhouser
(29) 1978 - Tri-Cities, WA - Ron Snyder - Dave Culley
(30) 1980 - Miami, FL - Dean Chenoweth - Dave Culley
(31) 1980 - Evansville, IN - Dean Chenoweth - Dave Culley
(32) 1980) - Detroit, MI - Dean Chenoweth - Dave Culley
(33) 1980 - Madison, IN - Dean Chenoweth - Dave Culley (GOLD CUP)
(34) 1980 - El Dorado, KS - Dean Chenoweth - Dave Culley
(35) 1981 - Miami, FL - Dean Chenoweth - Dave Culley
(36) 1981 - Detroit, MI - Dean Chenoweth - Dave Culley
(37) 1981 - Madison, IN - Dean Chenoweth - Dave Culley
(38) 1981- Seattle, WA - Dean Chenoweth - Dave Culley (GOLD CUP)
(39) 1981 - San Diego, CA - Dean Chenoweth - Dave Culley
(40) 1981 - Acapulco, Mexico - Dean Chenoweth - Dave Culley
(41) 1982 - Miami, FL - Dean Chenoweth - Dave Culley
(42) 1983 - Miami, FL - Jim Kropfeld - Dave Culley
(43) 1983 - Romulus, NY - Jim Kropfeld - Dave Culley
(44) 1983 - Madison, IN - Jim Kropfeld - Dave Culley
(45) 1983 - Seattle, WA - Jim Kropfeld - Dave Culley
(46) 1984 - Miami, FL - Jim Kropfeld - Dave Culley
(47) 1984 - Evansville, IN - Jim Kropfeld - Dave Culley

Madison -- Hydroplane Heritage - Fred Farley & Ron Harsin

(48) 1984 - Detroit, MI - Jim Kropfeld - Jeff Neff
(49) 1984 - Seattle, WA - Jim Kropfeld - Jeff Neff
(50) 1984 - San Diego, CA - Jim Kropfeld - Jeff Neff
(51) 1984 - Lake Ozark, MO - Jim Kropfeld - Jeff Neff
(52) 1985 - Syracuse, NY - Jim Kropfeld - Jeff Neff
(53) 1985 - San Diego, CA - Jim Kropfeld - Jeff Neff
(54) 1986 - Miami, FL - Jim Kropfeld - Ron Brown
(55) 1986 - Evansville, IN - Jim Kropfeld - Ron Brown
(56) 1986 - Las Vegas, NV - Jim Kropfeld - Ron Brown
(57) 1987 - Miami, FL - Jim Kropfeld - Ron Brown
(58) 1987 - Evansville, IN - Jim Kropfeld - Ron Brown
(59) 1987 - Madison, IN - Jim Kropfeld - Ron Brown
(60) 1987 - Tri-Cities, WA - Jim Kropfeld - Ron Brown
(61) 1987 - Seattle, WA - Jim Kropfeld - Ron Brown
(62) 1988 - Syracuse, NY - Tom D'Eath - Ron Brown
(63) 1988 - Tri-Cities, WA - Tom D'Eath - Ron Brown
(64) 1988 - Seattle, WA - Tom D'Eath - Ron Brown
(65) 1988 - Las Vegas, NV - Tom D'Eath - Ron Brown
(66) 1989 - Houston, TX - Jim Kropfeld - Ron Brown
(67) 1989 - Madison, IN - Jim Kropfeld - Ron Brown
(68) 1989 - Syracuse, NY - Tom D'Eath - Ron Brown
(69) 1989 - San Diego, CA - Tom D'Eath - Ron Brown (GOLD CUP)
(70) 1990 - Detroit, MI - Tom D'Eath - Ron Brown (GOLD CUP)
(71) 1990 - Evansville, IN - Tom D'Eath - Ron Brown
(72) 1990 - Syracuse, NY - Tom D'Eath - Ron Brown
(73) 1990 - Tri-Cities, WA - Tom D'Eath - Ron Brown
(74) 1990 - Kansas City, MO - Tom D'Eath - Ron Brown
(75) 1990 - Honolulu, HI - Tom D'Eath - Ron Brown
(76) 1991 - Evansville, IN - Scott Pierce - Ron Brown
(77) 1991 - Seattle, WA - Scott Pierce - Ron Brown
(78) 1991 - San Diego, CA - Scott Pierce - Ron Brown
(79) 1992 - Miami, FL - Chip Hanauer - Ron Brown
(80) 1992 - Detroit, MI - Chip Hanauer - Ron Brown (GOLD

Madison -- Hydroplane Heritage - Fred Farley & Ron Harsin

CUP)
(81) 1992 - Evansville, IN - Chip Hanauer - Ron Brown
(82) 1992 - Madison, IN - Chip Hanauer - Ron Brown
(83) 1992 - Tri-Cities, WA - Chip Hanauer - Ron Brown
(84) 1992 - Kansas City, MO - Chip Hanauer - Ron Brown
(85) 1992 - Honolulu, HI - Chip Hanauer - Ron Brown
(86) 1993 - Detroit, MI - Chip Hanauer - Ron Brown (GOLD CUP)
(87) 1993 - Miami, FL - Chip Hanauer - Ron Brown
(88) 1993 - Evansville, IN - Chip Hanauer - Ron Brown
(89) 1993 - Madison, In - Chip Hanauer - Ron Brown
(90) 1993 - Kansas City, MO - Chip Hanauer - Ron Brown
(91) 1993 - Tri-Cities, WA - Chip Hanauer - Ron Brown
(92) 1993 - Seattle, WA - Chip Hanauer - Ron Brown
(93) 1994 - Lewisville, TX - Mike Hanson - Ron Brown
(94) 1994 - Evansville, IN - Chip Hanauer - Ron Brown
(95) 1994 - Madison, IN - Chip Hanauer - Ron Brown
(96) 1994 - Tri-Cities, WA - Chip Hanauer - Ron Brown
(97) 1995 - Phoenix, AZ - Chip Hanauer - Ron Brown
(98) 1995 - Detroit, MI - Chip Hanauer - Ron Brown (GOLD CUP)
(99) 1995 - Lewisville, TX - Chip Hanauer - Ron Brown
(100) 1995 - Seattle, WA - Chip Hanauer - Ron Brown
(101) 1995 - Honolulu, HI - Chip Hanauer - Ron Brown
(102) 1996 - San Diego, CA - Mark Evans - Ron Brown
(103) 1996 - Honolulu, HI - Mark Evans - Ron Brown
(104) 1997 - Detroit, MI - Dave Villwock - Ron Brown (GOLD CUP)
(105) 1997 - Evansville, IN - Dave Villwock - Ron Brown
(106) 1997 - Madison, IN - Dave Villwock - Ron Brown
(107) 1997 - Norfolk, VA - Dave Villwock - Ron Brown
(108) 1997 - Las Vegas, NV - Mark Weber - Ron Brown
(109) 1998 - Evansville, IN - Dave Villwock - Mark Smith
(110) 1998 - Detroit, MI - Dave Villwock - Mark Smith (GOLD CUP)

(111) 1998 - Norfolk, VA - Dave Villwock - Mark Smith
(112) 1998 - Tri-Cities, WA - Dave Villwock - Mark Smith
(113) 1998 - Seattle, WA - Dave Villwock - Mark Smith
(114) 1998 - Madison, IN - Dave Villwock - Mark Smith
(115) 1998 - San Diego, CA - Dave Villwock - Mark Smith
(116) 1998 - Las Vegas, NV - Dave Villwock - Mark Smith
(117) 1999 - Barrie, Ontario - Dave Villwock - Mark Smith
(118) 1999 - Evansville, In - Dave Villwock - Mark Smith
(119) 1999 - Norfolk, VA - Dave Villwock - Mark Smith
(120) 1999 - Tri-Cities, WA - Dave Villwock - Mark Smith
(121) 1999 - Seattle, WA - Dave Villwock - Mark Smith
(122) 1999 - Kelowna, BC - Dave Villwock - Mark Smith
(123) 1999 - San Diego, CA - Dave Villwock - Mark Smith
(124) 1999 - Honolulu, HI - Dave Villwock - Mark Smith
(125) 2000 - Lake Havasu City, AZ - Dave Villwock - Mark Smith
(126) 2000 - Evansville, IN - Dave Villwock - Mark Smith
(127) 2000 - Madison, IN - Dave Villwock - Mark Smith
(128) 2000 - Detroit, MI - Dave Villwock - Mark Smith (GOLD CUP)
(129) 2000 - Seattle, WA - Dave Villwock - Mark Smith
(130) 2000 - San Diego, CA - Dave Villwock - Mark Smith
(131) 2001 - Evansville, IN - Dave Villwock - Mark Smith
(132) 2002 - Evansville, IN - Dave Villwock - Mark Smith
(133) 2002 - Detroit, MI - Dave Villwock - Mark Smith (GOLD CUP)
(134) 2002 - Seattle, WA - Dave Villwock - Mark Smith

Madison -- Hydroplane Heritage - Fred Farley & Ron Harsin

*The first MISS BUDWEISER a 4-seater hydro
Driven here by owner Bernie Little*

MISS BUDWEISER WORLD HIGH POINTS
CHAMPIONSHIPS(1969-2002)

(1) 1969 (7) 1984 (13) 1992 (19) 1999
(2) 1970 (8) 1986 (14) 1993 (20) 2000
(3) 1971 (9) 1987 (15) 1994 (21) 2001
(4) 1977 (10) 1988 (16) 1995 (22) 2002
(5) 1980 (11) 1989 (17) 1997
(6) 1981 (12) 1991 (18) 1998)

MISS BUDWEISER DRIVER VICTORIES
(1966-2002)

Dave Villwock (30) - 1997-2002
Dean Chenoweth (23) - 1970-1982
Jim Kropfeld (22) - 1983-1989
Chip Hanauer (22) - 1992-1995
Tom D'Eath (12) - 1988-1990
Mickey Remund (6) - 1975-1977
Bill Sterett (5) - 1968-1969
Howie Benns (3) - 1974
Scott Pierce (3) - 1991
Bill Brow (2) - 1966

Madison -- Hydroplane Heritage - Fred Farley & Ron Harsin

Mark Evans (2) - 1996
Mike Thomas (1) - 1967
Ron Snyder (1) - 1978
Mike Hanson (1) - 1994
Mark Weber (1) - 1997

MISS BUDWEISER CREW CHIEF VICTORIES (1966-2002)

Ron Brown (55) - 1986-1997
Mark Smith (26) - 1998-2002
Dave Culley (19) - 1978-1984
George McKernan (14) - 1966-1971
Tom Frankhouser (14) - 1973-1977
Jeff Neff (6) - 1984-1985

The MISS BUDWEISER that ran in the 1971 Madison Gold Cup race. Now rebuilt and on display at the Hydroplane and Race Boat Museum in Seattle, Washington.

Madison -- Hydroplane Heritage - Fred Farley & Ron Harsin

MISS BUDWEISER

The most recent MISS BUDWEISER
Winner of the 2002 Gold Cup race
Shown here at Madison, Indiana

Chapter Four
Madison, Indiana

Madison, Indiana could easily be separated into two towns instead of the single one that currently exists. There is the older, historic downtown area within the Ohio River valley and the second part, a modern sales center on top of the hill.

As the town developed over the past 50 years, individuals within the community realized the need to preserve the historical content of the downtown area. Plans were drawn and approved to keep the downtown area as a historical landmark while developing business and industry on the hilltop. Because of this, a visitor will find two communities within Madison, Indiana. The local residents know and refer to these areas as "the downtown" and "north Madison".

Over the years, Madison has enjoyed many "firsts" including:

* The steepest railroad grade in the world.
* The tallest smoke stacks in the world (IKE Clifty Creek Power Plant)
* The largest town in Indiana (years ago)
* The largest industrial base in Indiana
* Site of the state capitol for a short time

All of these "firsts" have come and gone. Madison has fallen from importance in the state economy and other towns have passed Madison in size and industry.

In 1784, the area which includes Madison, was ceded by Virginia to the United States Government and became part of the Northwest Territory.

In 1805, white settlers searched the area for home sites. The first cabin was built on Madison's hilltop in the spring of 1806 by Elder, Jessie Vawter. That same year William and John Hall arrived and erected their cabin near the river bank in what became the east end of the city.

A public sale of government land was held at Jeffersonville Indiana in 1809. Selling for $2.50 per acre, John Paul purchased the ground on which the city grew. Assisted by Jonathan Lyon and Lewis Davis, he laid out that portion of the budding city bounded by First, Fourth, East and West Streets. Since James Madison was currently President of the United States, John Paul named the town Madison in his honor.

Settlers began arriving by boat from New England and the east. Others trekked up from the south via the Cumberland Gap. In addition to bringing their cherished possessions they bore in mind the image of architectural customs of the localities from which they came. Substantial houses of brick and stone began rising beside their log neighbors. No single architectural style predominated and this heritage of Georgian, Federal, Regency, Classic revival, Gothic and Americanized Italian Villa architectural styles became unique to southern Indiana.

With the river traffic, Madison grew quickly to become the largest town in the state of Indiana. Its industrial strength was derived from its river port and meat processing plant. As the years progressed, Madison's importance would diminish and other towns within the state would grow. Trucking, rail and other forms of transportation would reduce the need for river traffic and, ultimately, the river port and the meat packing industry would both cease operations in Madison.

Within Madison, the Jeremiah Sullivan house is open to the public. The house is a Federal style home built in 1818. The home has been restored by the Madison Historical Society and is dedicated to the man who gave Indianapolis its name.

The James F.D. Lanier home stands on Second Street in Madison. This home is now a state memorial which honors Mr. Lanier as a patriot and financier for his part during the Civil War. Mr. Lanier advanced Governor Morton $400,000 during the Civil War to equip ten thousand Indiana soldiers. Two years later, when the state legislature adjourned without making appropriations to meet the state expenses, Mr. Lanier again provided the state of Indiana with a $640,000 loan.

As a state memorial, the Lanier home is run by Indiana State Parks and is open to the public.

The years leading up to the Civil War saw Madison as a route along the Underground Railroad for runaway slaves. The individuals living within the town had mixed feelings. Some supported the Northern Union, while others supported the Southern Confederacy.

The story is told of one man in Madison who helped runaway slaves along the underground railroad, while his brother was active in searching for and returning runaway slaves for their bounty.

During the Civil War, Madison was the home of the largest Union hospital east of the Mississippi River. This hospital was located at the west end of the city where the Country Club is now. At the end of the war, many of the small dwellings that were used by the hospital to house Union soldiers were sold and moved to different locations. These small dwellings are still used today as homes of many Madison residents and can be seen while driving down Main Street on the west end of town.

During the 1940's, Madison and the rest of the nation were involved with World War II. The federal government seized a 55,000 acre parcel of land just north of Madison and turned it into an Army ammunition testing facility. Through WW II, the Korean war and Viet-Nam war, this facility tested millions of rounds of ammunition for our armed forces. With the military cutbacks under the Clinton administration, the Jefferson Proving Ground was closed. Today it has been turned over to the U.S. Fish and Wildlife service to be transformed into the largest wildlife reserve east of the Mississippi River. Big Oaks Wildlife Reserve is open to the public on a limited basis and is home to a wide variety of wildlife.

In 1943, during World War II, Madison was picked by the Office of War Information as a "typical American town." Movies were made of the town and had global distribution. The movies were shown to tired and weary soldiers in the battle areas who were told "places like this back home" are what you are fighting for.

The movie "Madison" is not the first time the town was used for the creation of a major motion picture. In 1958, Madison was the setting for the filming of a movie called "Some Came Running". The movie starred Frank Sinatra, Dean Martin and Shirley MacLaine.

Madison -- Hydroplane Heritage - Fred Farley & Ron Harsin

No one within the Madison community will forget the date, April 3rd, 1974. On this date, hundreds of tornadoes destroyed property and homes across the midwest. Many people were killed and thousands more injured as the killer tornadoes struck. Jefferson County was just one place that felt the full force of the storm. An F4 killer destroyed the town of Hanover, Hanover College, the Indiana-Kentucky Electric (Clifty Creek) Power Plant, the Madison State Hospital, North Madison, every school within the county and wreaked total destruction upon the Madison hilltop district. Nearly every residence on the Madison hilltop was destroyed along with a majority of the hilltop businesses. Lives were lost and it was a sad time for the community. However, it showed how strong the people of the community really are. The destruction brought out the best in neighbors and all worked together to rebuild.

For the first time in years, Madison was unable to host the Madison Regatta on the 4th of July weekend. However, the community banded together, worked hard on the destruction cleanup effort and would come back strong to hold the regatta on October 13th of that year.

In 1977 Madison had the honor of being picked as one of three winners within the nation to participate in the Main Street U.S.A. project. The program, sponsored by the National Trust for Historic Preservation and the United States Chamber of Commerce, provided funds to restore older buildings along Main Street to their original condition. This gave the town a face lift, while preserving it's historical heritage.

Madison, today is still very much an important sales center for burley tobacco. Sales run from 17 to 19 million dollars a season, with 9 to 11 million pounds of tobacco crossing the floors of the three tobacco warehouses. Madison's tobacco market is supplied by growers throughout Southern Indiana and Northern Kentucky.

River boats and small pleasure craft provide recreation on the Ohio River. Coal barges travel the river on a daily basis. The water route now handles a larger volume of cargo annually than clears through the Panama Canal.

In the movie, "Madison", the town is called "obsolete". In a way, it is, in another way it's not. It's a matter of perspective. However, if you are looking for a quiet community with a low crime rate, where neighbors still know each other and children can play outdoors safely, then Madison and the surrounding communities are a very nice place to live. The town offers a slow "old man river" relaxed pace with modern shopping centers and industrial manufacturing plants just a few minutes away.

Madison -- Hydroplane Heritage - *Fred Farley & Ron Harsin*

The Madison, Indiana Courthouse

*The Madison Broadway Fountain
as shown in the movie, "Madison"*

Madison -- Hydroplane Heritage - Fred Farley & Ron Harsin

One of the water jets on the fountain

*A Madison, Indiana landmark, the Ohio Theater
Or as the movie said, "the thee-a-tor"*

Madison -- Hydroplane Heritage - Fred Farley & Ron Harsin

Main Street

Main Street

The building in the middle of the picture with the clock in front of it is the "Madison Bank and Trust Company" which is featured in the movie, "Madison."

Madison -- Hydroplane Heritage - Fred Farley & Ron Harsin

The Ohio River front

The Ohio River front has been the site of the Madison Regatta for years. In recent years, it has been upgraded to a park like setting.

Madison -- Hydroplane Heritage - Fred Farley & Ron Harsin

The Madison/Milton Bridge. Finished in 1929, it stands over the hydroplane race course.

Madison -- Hydroplane Heritage - Fred Farley & Ron Harsin

The Madison Regatta Hydroplane Officials Stand.

The Ohio River, from nearby Hanover College.

Hanover College landmark

Hanover College north entrance in winter

Madison -- Hydroplane Heritage - Fred Farley & Ron Harsin

Hanover College Clock Tower in winter

Madison Angel

Chapter Five
History of Hydroplane Racing in Madison, Indiana

Ohio River Thunder
A Hydroplane Heritage

The Ohio River Valley has been a hotbed of hydroplane activity for much of this century. In the post-World War II era, more Unlimited races have been run on the Ohio River than on any other venue. Currently, the towns of Evansville and Madison in southern Indiana host the Thunderboats as part of the American Power Boat Association's annual tour.

During the first decade after the war, the Unlimiteds also raced at Louisville, Kentucky, Cincinnati, Ohio, New Martinsville, West Virginia and Pittsburgh, Pennsylvania. Many of the Ohio River races of the 1940s and '50s were one-heat, multi-class free-for-alls, a format of competition that has long since vanished from the Unlimited scene.

From 1969 to 1978, the U-boats ran at Owensboro for the Kentucky Governor's Cup, an event that was replaced on the Thunderboat schedule by Evansville's first "Thunder On The Ohio" in 1979.

One of the most famous Ohio River hydroplanes was the HOOSIER BOY, a Liberty-powered step hydro, which was obviously patterned after Gar Wood's MISS AMERICA boats. HOOSIER BOY represented Rising Sun, Indiana, a small town located about 50 miles upriver from Madison.

In 1924, HOOSIER BOY set a never-to-be-equaled long-distance record from Cincinnati to Louisville and back to Cincinnati. Owner/driver J.W. Whitlock covered the 260 Ohio River miles at just a shade under 60 miles per hour.

The show category of inboard racing in the 1930s was the popular, 725 Cubic Inch Class of the Mississippi Valley Power Boat Association. Comparable to the American Power Boat Association's Gold Cup Class, the 725s used the venerable Hispano-Suiza ("Hisso") engine from the Spad aircraft of World War I.

Boat racing in Madison, Indiana in 1930. The boats ran in the opposite direction from today's races.

Three of the more popular campaigners in the 725 Class were "Wild Bill" Cantrell's WHY WORRY, Marion Cooper's MERCURY and George Davis's HERMES IV (the future IT'S A WONDER).

Madison -- Hydroplane Heritage - Fred Farley & Ron Harsin

IT'S A WONDER

The mile straightaway record for 725s was set at 98 miles per hour by MERCURY at Washington, D.C., in 1940. Then, an hour later, WHY WORRY went out and raised the record to 99.

With the advent of World War II and gasoline rationing, power boat racing was suspended for the duration. Two of the first Ohio River races to be run after the war were the 1946 Viking Trophy at New Martinsville, won by Lou Fageol in SO-LONG. The 1947 Marine Derby Regatta at Louisville, was won by George Davis in HERMES V.

HERMES V

After World War II, the Gold Cup Class and the 725 Class combined and changed over to the Unlimited Class. By doing so, they could take advantage of the huge supply of Allison and Rolls-Royce Merlin aircraft engines developed for the war effort.

New Martinsville was a popular stop-over for the Unlimiteds for nearly a decade. It was cancelled after 1954 when a determination was made that the river was too narrow for the modern boats to safely compete.

Madison had no such problem and has been an Unlimited mainstay since 1950. The first Indiana Governor's Cup was offered in 1951. It was won by Marion Cooper in the 225 Cubic Inch Class HORNET. The first Unlimited race at Madison to count for APBA National High Points was in 1954. Bill Cantrell won at the wheel of Joe Schoenith's GALE IV.

The first Ohio River heat at over 100 miles per hour was run by Danny Foster in 1955 at Madison with Guy Lombardo's TEMPO VII. Two years later, Bill Muncey set a world heat record of 112.312 with MISS THRIFTWAY, also at Madison. The record stood for six years.

The first turbine-powered hydroplane to win an Ohio River race was Fran Muncey's ATLAS VAN LINES in 1984 at Madison. With Chip Hanauer driving, the ATLAS was the first truly competitive turbine boat in the APBA Unlimited Class.

The all-time high water mark of Ohio River Thunderboat racing had to be the fabulous, 1971 Madison Regatta covered in Chapter Eight.

History Of The Madison Regatta

Madison, Indiana, is steeped in a competitive tradition that dates back to the 1800s when steamboats raced each other on the legendary Ohio River. Perhaps because of this, boat racing is very deeply engrained in the public consciousness.

According to folklore, one of the earliest boat races to occur in the vicinity of Madison was a keelboat competition that supposedly matched Mike Fink, the flamboyant "King of the River," with Davy Crockett, "King of the Wild Frontier." Crockett emerged the winner (by barely a boat length) in the apocryphal race that began in Maysville, Kentucky and ended in New Orleans, Louisiana.

The earliest documented power boat regatta at Madison took place in 1911. The steamship PRINCESS from Coney Island anchored in the middle of the river. Power launches ran an oval track, roughly, around the boat. This was also one of the earliest examples of competition as it is currently characterized around a closed course.

The first boats to be specifically built for racing appeared in 1919. Among these was the famous DAYTON KID, a step hydroplane, owned by Pat Parrish.

The first major regatta to be run in Madison occurred in 1929 under the auspices of the Ohio Valley Motorboat Racing Association of Cincinnati. L.J. Montifer's CATHERINE III emerged as the champion that Labor Day weekend. Equipped with a 1914, vintage Hispano-Suiza ("Hisso") aircraft engine, the craft won $400 for its victories in the 725 Cubic Inch Class race and the Hydroplane Free-For-All around the approximate 2-1/2-mile course.

The driver with the most wins at Madison during the years between the World Wars was popular "Wild Bill" Cantrell of Louisville. Cantrell, who would become a racing legend in the post-war Unlimited Class, won the 725 Class title three times in 1934 and 1935 with BIG SHOT and in 1936 with WHY WORRY.

WHY WORRY

The disastrous Ohio River flood of 1937 brought down the curtain on organized boat racing in Madison. Competition did not resume until 1949 when a local group, which later became Madison Regatta, Inc., staged an unsanctioned "wildcat" affair for Limited inboard and outboard racing craft. The largest class to participate in 1949 was the 225 Cubic Inch hydroplanes. The winner of the 225 Class race was the

HORNET, driven by Marion Cooper of Louisville, who in 1961 would achieve fame as the original driver of the community-owned MISS MADISON Unlimited hydroplane.

The Madison Regatta entered the modern era in 1950, which was the first year an American Power Boat Association (APBA) sanction was in effect. It was also the first Madison race to be attended by a modern Unlimited hydroplane, MY DARLING. She posted a winning average speed of 76.000 miles per hour with owner, Andy Marcy from Springfield, Illinois, at the wheel.

The inaugural running of the Indiana Governor's Cup was the highlight of the 1951 Madison Regatta. Marion Cooper's HORNET claimed this first in a long line of Governor's Cup races at a speed of 65.886. Also participating in 1951 were the Unlimited Class GALE II, driven by Lee Schoenith and the 725 Class IT'S A WONDER, handled by George Davis.

All of the Unlimited races run at Madison between 1950 and 1953 were multi-class events that consisted of a single heat and didn't count for APBA National High Points. The first race to count toward National Points was the 1954 Indiana Governor's Cup, which was won by Bill Cantrell driving Joe Schoenith's Allison-powered GALE IV from Detroit.

From 1954 onward, the Madison Unlimited race has always been scheduled for two or more heats with National High Points at stake. The tiny Ohio River town of 13,000 was now in the major league of water sports.

The first heat at over 100 miles per hour in Madison history occurred in 1955. Danny Foster, the Governor's Cup winner that year with bandleader Guy Lombardo's TEMPO VII, averaged 102.079 with an Allison engine.

GALE II

Bill Muncey became the first three-time consecutive winner of the Indiana Governor's Cup in 1960-61-62 with MISS THRIFTWAY (also known as MISS CENTURY 21). This occurred on the same race course where Muncey almost lost his life in a spectacular crash while driving an earlier MISS THRIFTWAY in the 1957 Madison Regatta.

Another three-time consecutive winner was Bill Harrah's TAHOE MISS, which won the 1964 and 1965 races with Chuck Thompson as driver and the 1966 race with Mira Slovak.

Bernie Little, the sport's most successful participant, first raced at Madison in 1963 with a remodeled former pleasure boat named TEMPO. Little's first in a long line of MISS BUDWEISER hydroplanes appeared in 1964, although his first Madison victory didn't occur until 1970. That was the year Dean Chenoweth did the honors after a head-to-head battle in the Final Heat with Leif Borgersen in NOTRE DAME.

Years later, in 1999, a Hollywood motion picture re-created the 1971 Gold Cup which was filmed on location in southern Indiana. The movie, titled "MADISON", staring actor, Jim Caviezel in the role of Jim McCormick, is currently scheduled for release in the near future.

The first turbine-powered hydroplane to win a

Madison race was Fran Muncey's ATLAS VAN LINES in 1984. With Chip Hanauer driving, the ATLAS was the first, truly competitive turbine boat in the APBA Unlimited Class. As a result of the 1984 Madison Regatta, the large-scale transition from Allison or Rolls-Royce piston power to Lycoming turbine power was inevitable.

The Madison Regatta has elevated the picturesque Ohio River town into a national sports arena. It does prove what can be accomplished when public-spirited citizens from all walks of life band together to stage an exciting production that gains nationwide, favorable publicity for an area.

Chip Hanauer

The Madison Regatta: The 1950s

For 50 years, the city of Madison, Indiana, has played host to "Water Racing's Greatest Show," the Unlimited hydroplanes -- the Thunderboats of the racing world.

Since 1950, the mighty Unlimiteds have occupied center stage at the annual Madison Regatta. The picturesque Ohio River town of 13,000 is second only to Detroit, Michigan, in the number of Thunderboat races run in consecutive years.

The Motor City has been on the Unlimited calendar every year since 1946. But the current sponsoring organization in Detroit wasn't founded until 1962.

A local Madison group staged an unsanctioned "wildcat" race in the fall of 1949 for Limited inboard and outboard hydroplanes. This same group, which is now known as Madison Regatta, Inc., applied for an American Power Boat Association (APBA) sanction in 1950. The sanction was granted and the precedent for the next 50 years was set.

HOOSIER BOY

In the last half-century, Madison, Indiana, has become one of the three traditional Unlimited hydroplane race sites, together with Detroit and Seattle, Washington, which started in 1951.

Many other small towns climbed on the Unlimited bandwagon during the decade of the 1950s. These included: New Martinsville, West Virginia; Elizabeth City, North Carolina; Dale Hollow, Tennessee; Windsor, Ontario; Picton, Ontario; Polson, Montana; Chelan, Washington and St. Clair, Michigan. None of these lasted more than a few years on the circuit.

The first Unlimited hydroplane to race at Madison was the MY DARLING, from Springfield, Illinois. Powered by a 12-cylinder Allison and driven by owner Andy Marcy, MY

Madison -- Hydroplane Heritage - Fred Farley & Ron Harsin

DARLING was a step hydro and did not have sponsons. Marcy defeated a field of smaller inboard hydroplanes at an average speed of 76.000 miles per hour. Phil Rothenbusch finished second to MY DARLING in WILD GOOSE, while J.D. Smith ran third with Y-39. Thom Cooper dropped out while leading in TOPS VII when a piece of driftwood lodged itself in the water intake.

Jim Noonan, of Louisville, served as APBA Referee at the 1950 Madison Regatta. Years later, his sons Mike and Billy Noonan would follow in their father's footsteps as Madison Unlimited referees.

The first four Unlimited races at Madison consisted of one heat of 15 miles in length on a 3-mile course and did not count for National High Points. These were essentially "free-for-all" races in which Limited hydroplanes could also participate.

A perpetual trophy for the Indiana Governor's Cup was introduced in 1951. The trophy could be won outright by any owner registering three victories with a 7-Litre or larger class of hull. Two boats of that description appeared in 1951: the Unlimited Class GALE II driven by Lee Schoenith and the 725 Class IT'S A WONDER handled by George Davis. Due to the sparseness of the field, boats from the smaller classes were invited by the race committee to "step-up" to race for the Governor's Cup. These included the HORNET, a 266 Class hull, owned and driven by Marion Cooper of Louisville. HORNET ultimately won the race at 65.886 when the larger boats experienced mechanical difficulties.

The 1952 and 1953 Indiana Governor's Cups were dominated by a 7-Litre Class hydroplane, the WILDCATTER, owned and driven by the father and son team of Burnett Bartley, Sr. and Jr., from Pittsburgh. Oliver Elam and the 7-Litre MERCURY ran second to Bartley, Jr., in 1952, while Ralph Manning in the Gold Cup Class OLLIE'S FOLLY finished runner-up in 1953. Claiming the third-place prize on both occasions was IT'S A WONDER with owner/driver George Davis twice duplicating his 1951 performance in the Hisso-powered, pre-war contender from Vine Grove, Kentucky.

As the first two-time consecutive winner in Governor's Cup history, WILDCATTER posted average speeds of 70.866 and 71.599.

Beginning in 1954, the Madison Regatta's main event became an exclusive Unlimited affair. This was also the first year in which a multi-heat format was used and APBA National High Points were at stake in the Indiana Governor's Cup.

Popular "Wild Bill" Cantrell won the 1954 race with Joe Schoenith's GALE IV, an Allison-powered craft from Detroit. Cantrell won the Final Heat at 91.556 in spite of a large hole in the port sponson, followed by Jack Bartlow in DORA MY SWEETIE, Lee Schoenith in GALE V and Bud Saile in MISS CADILLAC.

Cantrell's 1954 victory was his fourth in Madison. Previously, in the 725 Class era, Bill had won the top prize with BIG SHOT in 1934 and 1935 and with WHY WORRY in 1936.

The first heat to be timed at over 100 miles per hour in Ohio River history was recorded in Heat One of the 1955 Governor's Cup. Danny Foster did the honors with bandleader, Guy Lombardo's TEMPO VII, a Les Staudacher-designed hull, at a speed of 102.079.

Rain postponed the 1955 race for two weeks. Foster won all three heats and was, clearly, the class of the field. For the benefit of the spectators, Danny throttled way down to 84.945 and 84.230 in Heats Two and Three to outdistance second-place GALE V over the finish line by a narrow margin.

Speeds were down in 1956 but the reliability was extraordinary with all five boats finishing all three heats. Fred

Madison -- Hydroplane Heritage - Fred Farley & Ron Harsin

Alter, driving the original MISS U.S. 1, placed second, first and first to claim the first of two Indiana Governor's Cups for owner George Simon.

Bud Saile's twin-Allison-powered MISS WAYNE took an overall second and scored an unexpected victory over Alter in Heat One by an incredible six feet at the finish line.

Third-place that year went to Doc Terry in Horace Dodge, Jr.'s DORA MY SWEETIE, followed by Marv Henrich's WHA HOPPEN TOO and Gordon Deneau's WHAT A PICKLE.

Record speeds and a record entry list highlighted the 1957 classic. This year saw Jack Regas score a sensational victory over eight other contenders with Edgar Kaiser's "Pink Lady" HAWAII KAI III.

The KAI was arguably the best race boat of the 1950s and was the epitome of the all-conquering Ted Jones design.

Regas posted a three-heat, 45-mile average of 106.061. Rookie Bob Schroeder in the former GALE IV (renamed WILDROOT CHARLIE) was runner-up. Defending champion, Alter, checked in third with a second-edition MISS U.S. 1.

The most spectacular performance of the weekend was the incredible showing by Bill Muncey in the original MISS THRIFTWAY. On Saturday, September 28, in Heat 1-A, the Willard Rhodes entry from Seattle turned an unprecedented 112.312, a world competition record for the 15-mile distance that would stand until 1963.

MISS U.S. I

Madison -- *Hydroplane Heritage* - *Fred Farley & Ron Harsin*

On Sunday, September 29, however, the newly crowned speed champion was a splintered wreck and the driver was badly injured. MISS THRIFTWAY had disintegrated while leading in Heat 2-A at 160 miles per hour at the start of lap two. MISS WAHOO pilot Mira Slovak saw the accident, stopped his boat and went to the aid of the stricken Muncey.

The 1958 and 1959 races were lean years, both in the number of participating boats and in the area of regatta finances.

When one less than the minimum number of four entries was received in 1958, industrialist Samuel F. DuPont came to the city's rescue with his new and unprepared NITROGEN from Wilmington, Delaware. With assistance from other boat crews, the DuPont craft did more than just start the race. It finished in second-place and scored a victory in the Final Heat with MISS SUPERTEST II pilot Bob Hayward pinch-hitting in the cockpit. Redheaded, Don Wilson and MISS U.S. I were the overall Governor's Cup winners with 1100 points, compared to NITROGEN's 925. Then came Slovak in MISS BARDAHL and Schroeder in WILDROOT CHARLIE.

Two years later, Mr. DuPont would make an outright gift of the NITROGEN to the city of Madison. This boat became the original, community-owned MISS MADISON in 1961.

A quartet of challengers appeared for the 1959 regatta. The late great Ron Musson in his first season as an Unlimited hydroplane jockey took all three heats at an average speed of 102.939 aboard HAWAII KAI III, which was owned at that time by Joe Mascari of New York. DuPont's NITROGEN finished runner-up again but with Norm Evans at the controls this time, ahead of Bill Brow in MISS BARDAHL and Bob Gilliam in KOLroy.

NITROGEN

Helping out on the HAWAII KAI crew in 1959 was Musson's good friend Graham Heath of Madison. Heath later served as crew chief of MISS MADISON from 1961 to 1965 and of MY GYPSY from 1966 to 1968.

Two months prior to the 1960 Indiana Governor's Cup, the regatta was badly in debt and in immediate need of administrative surgery. Leadership of the race decided that private capital was needed to keep Madison on the Unlimited calendar. A $5000 bank loan, over 20 local groups and 150 individual members all figured in the organizational retrenchment. It proved to be the salvation of the Madison Regatta.

The 1960 race was run as scheduled and so were the next 40 years of races at Madison, in a tradition that continues to the present day.

The Madison Regatta: The 1960s

The 1960s were a decade of change in Unlimited hydroplane racing. Cash prizes became mandatory. Boats with commercial names, rather than nicknames, became the rule not the exception.

The Madison Regatta, having been plagued in recent years with financial woes and sparse entry lists, had its administrative house in order in 1960 and was back on firm financial footing. Eight Unlimiteds showed up in 1960, compared to only four in 1958 and 1959.

Bill Muncey became the first, three-time consecutive winning driver in Indiana Governor's Cup history in 1960-61-62 with MISS THRIFTWAY. A Ted Jones-designed hull, the persimmon and white MISS THRIFTWAY was renamed MISS CENTURY 21 during 1961-62 to publicize the 1962 Seattle World's Fair.

Ted Jones

During those three pinnacle years, Muncey entered nine heats at Madison, won eight of them and finished second once. He was also National High Point Champion during those same years.

Ron Musson claimed the runner-up honor twice during the MISS THRIFTWAY era. He did it in 1960 with NITROGEN TOO and in 1962 with MISS BARDAHL. Both were new boats in their first year of racing.

Bill Cantrell took second-place in 1961 with GALE V and was the only driver to ever defeat the victorious MISS CENTURY 21 in a heat of competition on the Ohio River.

The 1961 and 1962 races featured the added attraction of a hometown entry when the first, community-owned MISS MADISON made her debut. A gift to the city from Sam DuPont, the three-year-old former NITROGEN took fourth in an eleven-boat field the first year and third in a ten-boat contingent the next time around. Driver, Marion Cooper and crew chief, Graham Heath did a fine job on a shoestring budget in a sport dominated by millionaires.

A new, Indiana Governor's Cup perpetual award was offered in 1963, when the previous trophy became the permanent possession of MISS THRIFTWAY/MISS CENTURY 21 owner Willard Rhodes after his third win the previous year. In accordance with Governor's Cup rules, the trophy could be won outright by any owner who scored three victories.

Bill Brow won the initial contest for the replacement cup with MISS EXIDE, owned by Milo and Glen Stoen. He ran a speed of 106.754 miles per hour for the three 15-mile heats. Bill Cantrell and GALE V took second-place but posted the fastest 45-mile average of the day with a speed of 106.867 around the 3-mile oval course.

MISS BARDAHL ran third in 1963 with Don Wilson substituting for Ron Musson. Ron had been injured several days earlier when he flipped the "Green Dragon" during a practice run.

Walt Kade finished fourth with BLUE CHIP, followed by George "Buddy" Byers and the former NITROGEN TOO, which was in its first race as the second MISS MADISON.

This was after the original MISS MADISON had been destroyed at the 1963 APBA Gold Cup Regatta on the Detroit River, two months earlier. MISS MADISON the second would continue to carry the City of Madison's banner into competition through the 1971 racing season. Her drivers would include Byers (1963, 64, 65), Jim McCormick (1966, 69, 70, 71) and Ed O'Halloran (1967, 68).

The 1963 Madison Regatta is significant as the only Unlimited hydroplane race ever driven by Indy car legend Eddie Sachs. Sachs took a turn at the wheel of Jack Schafer's huge twin-Allison-powered SUCH CRUST IV. He finished seventh in a ten-boat field at Madison. Eddie planned to return the following year with the Schafer team, but this was not to be. Sachs was fatally injured in a fiery crash at the 1964 Indianapolis "500."

Casino owner Bill Harrah from Reno, Nevada, became the second owner in four years to retire the Governor's Cup with three consecutive wins. His TAHOE MISS proved to be the class of a thirteen-boat field in 1964, a fourteen-boat gathering in 1965 and a ten-boat contingent in 1966.

Driver Chuck Thompson claimed the first two victories at 105.372 and 105.503 respectively, while his successor Mira Slovak tied down the third leg of the trophy racing with a speed of 97.790.

Cantrell was runner-up again in 1964 with the new MISS SMIRNOFF, owned by the Gale Enterprises team from Detroit. "Wild Bill" won the Final Heat at 105.633, followed by TAHOE MISS at 101.963 and Byers in MISS MADISON at 101.332.

Musson, nearing the end of his brilliant career, posted the fastest heat of the 1965 race with MISS BARDAHL at 106.867. Musson and Thompson both won their respective preliminary heats and were rated as co-favorites for the Governor's Cup going into the Final Heat. MISS BARDAHL, however, was penalized an extra lap for an illegal lane change and had to settle for second-place overall.

An accident involving popular, Bill Cantrell marred the 1965 regatta when MISS SMIRNOFF encountered the wake of an illegally moving MISS LAPEER at the start of Heat 2-A. Cantrell lost control when the boat fell into a "hole" and he was pitched into the water. Incredibly, no official action was taken against MISS LAPEER pilot, Warner Gardner who had caused the mishap. "Wild Bill" recovered from his injuries and continued as a driver for another three years.

Sadly, the 1965 Madison Regatta marked the final

Madison -- Hydroplane Heritage - Fred Farley & Ron Harsin

Ohio River appearance of several of the sport's most respected chauffeurs.

Chuck Thompson was killed driving SMIRNOFF at the 1966 Gold Cup in Detroit.

Ron Musson suffered fatal injuries in an accident at the 1966 President's Cup in Washington, D.C., while driving a revolutionary, new cabover MISS BARDAHL.

Rex Manchester died on the same day as Musson when NOTRE DAME collided with Don Wilson driving the MISS BUDWEISER. Wilson was also killed.

Thompson, Musson and Wilson, among the three of them, accounted for four Indiana Governor's Cup victories in 1958-59-64-65. Manchester had finished third in the 1965 Madison Regatta with NOTRE DAME.

In the 1966 Governor's Cup race, Slovak and TAHOE MISS took second-place in Heat-1 to Gardner and MISS LAPEER. Mira rebounded to beat the LAPEER in Heat-2 and Heat-3 to claim the title.

The new MY GYPSY, owned and driven by Jim Ranger, took third in 1966. One of the most popular race boats of the 1960s, the GYPSY had Madisonian, Graham Heath in the role of crew chief.

After finishing ninth in the 1965 Governor's Cup, the community-owned MISS MADISON qualified for the Final Heat and finished fourth overall in 1966 with rookie Unlimited jockey, Jim McCormick in the cockpit. McCormick had scored a victory in a Limited race at the 1964 Madison Regatta as driver of the 266 Cubic Inch Class hydroplane, MISS KATHLEEN.

The Madison race course was shortened from 3 miles to 2-1/2 miles in 1967 in the interest of improving spectator vantage points. Also, for the first time in the post-World War II era, the regatta was contested in early July instead of September or October. This established a scheduling precedent that has stood ever since. With the exceptions of

1974 and 1998, all of the Unlimited races run at Madison since 1967 have coincided with the Fourth of July weekend.

Billy Schumacher made his competitive debut at Madison in 1967 aboard the new Ed Karelsen-designed MISS BARDAHL. Schumacher had been the late Musson's hand-picked successor as driver for owner, Ole Bardahl's Seattle-based team, which had never before won at Madison.

"Billy the Schu" achieved championship results in both the 1967 and 1968 Indiana Governor's Cup contests. At age 24, Schumacher was one of the youngest winners in Madison Regatta history. He was already a veteran of the Unlimited wars, having handled CUTIE RADIO and MISS TOOL CRIB in 1961 and $ BILL in 1963-64. Billy had also test-driven the ill-fated cabover MISS BARDAHL during the 1966 pre-season.

MISS BARDAHL posted heat finishes of second, first and first in 1967 to outscore second-place Chuck Hickling in HARRAH'S CLUB (the former TAHOE MISS), 1100 points to 925. This was in the days when winners were determined on the basis of total points, rather than the order of finish in a winner-take-all Final Heat, as it is today.

Jim Ranger took third in 1967 with MY GYPSY, followed by fourth-place, Jim McCormick with Bob Fendler's WAYFARERS CLUB LADY.

Schumacher and MISS BARDAHL had to work for the victory in 1968. Jack Regas and NOTRE DAME had decisively beaten them in Heat-2 and had set a course record of 104.026 for the 15-mile distance that was to stand for the next five years.

Then, in the Final Heat, Schumacher made a bad start and had to "catch-up" for four laps before finally overtaking the front-running NOTRE DAME.

Warner Gardner and MISS EAGLE ELECTRIC wound up second on points to MISS BARDAHL at Madison in 1968. MISS EAGLE ELECTRIC had spent six lackluster seasons, starting in 1962, as Bill Schuyler's $ BILL. Since being acquired by future PAY 'n PAK owner Dave Heerensperger, the "Screaming Eagle" had come alive and was the scourge of the Unlimited Class.

WAYFARERS CLUB LADY

Gardner and MISS EAGLE ELECTRIC won three races in 1968. He was in contention at the Gold Cup in Detroit when the boat took a bad bounce and cartwheeled itself to pieces. MISS EAGLE ELECTRIC was destroyed and Gardner was fatally injured.

An added highlight of the 1968 Madison Regatta was the first of two contests for the Richard C. Heck Memorial Trophy, named after a recently deceased past-president of the regatta. The one-heat race was for boats not qualifying for the Final Heat of the Governor's Cup.

Tommy "Tucker" Fults won the inaugural running of the Heck Memorial with MY GYPSY and repeated in 1970 with PAY 'n PAK'S, 'LIL BUZZARD.

Dean Chenoweth followed Billy Schumacher's lead with a pair of back-to-back victories of his own in 1969 and 1970 at the controls of MYR'S SPECIAL and MISS BUDWEISER.

Dean had been a youthful spectator at the 1954

Madison Regatta when Bill Cantrell won the top award with GALE IV. Fifteen years later, Chenoweth himself was the Indiana Governor's Cup champion, astride a contemporary Gale Enterprises hull with none other than Cantrell as his team manager.

MISS U.S. with Bill Muncey driving finished second in 1969 while MISS MADISON ran third with "Gentleman Jim" McCormick back in the cockpit, occupied the two previous seasons by Ed O'Halloran.

The nine-boat field in 1969 also included (in the order of finish) Bill Sterett, Sr., in MISS BUDWEISER, Tommy Fults in MISS OWENSBORO, Earl Wham in ATLAS VAN LINES, Leif Borgersen in NOTRE DAME, Mike Wolfbauer in MY CUPIEE and Walt Kade in SAVAIR'S MIST.

Chenoweth's winning averages were 96.131 with MYR'S SPECIAL and 95.761 with MISS BUDWEISER.

The City of Madison had been in the Unlimited hydroplane racing business for twenty consecutive years. Only Detroit, Michigan and Washington, D.C., which first appeared on the Unlimited calendar in 1946, had hosted more races than Madison.

The Madison Regatta: The 1970s

By the 1970s, Unlimited hydroplane racing had professionalized itself. A sport that had previously been little more than a rich man's hobby was now a full-fledged commercial pursuit.

A landmark tax case in 1963, involving George Simon's MISS U.S. racing team, had established an important precedent. The IRS had upheld Simon's contention that Unlimited racing was a legitimate business expense within specified guidelines and thereby tax deductible.

This ruling opened the door to major corporate sponsorship on a scale undreamed of in the past. One of the

Madison -- Hydroplane Heritage - Fred Farley & Ron Harsin

first corporations to make a sizeable commitment to Unlimited racing was Anheuser-Busch, which introduced the first, in a long line of MISS BUDWEISER hydroplanes in 1964.

By 1970, the Unlimiteds were the showcase of the power boat racing world and drew more spectators than any other category. In the quarter of a century since the end of World War II, the boats themselves had evolved remarkably. However, the engines of choice were still the Allison and the Rolls-Royce Merlin. These engines, originally intended for use in WWII fighter planes, were now in short supply.

Automotive power had been tried in the Unlimited ranks and found wanting. Turbine power loomed as a definite possibility but was largely dismissed as science fiction when the 1970s dawned.

The first Madison Regatta of the new decade saw Dean Chenoweth of Xenia, Ohio, repeat as Indiana Governor's Cup champion with Bernie Little's MISS BUDWEISER. Chenoweth had won the 1969 Governor's Cup with Joe Schoenith's MYR'S SPECIAL.

Billy Sterett, Jr., finished second in the 1970 Madison race with MISS OWENSBORO, which was the former automotive-powered, MISS CHRYSLER CREW, now repowered with an Allison engine borrowed from MY GYPSY. Then came Leif Borgersen in NOTRE DAME, Bill Muncey in MYR SHEET METAL and Jim McCormick in MISS MADISON.

NOTRE DAME was an early leader in the Final Heat with MISS BUDWEISER in hot pursuit. Then Chenoweth moved ahead of Borgersen on lap-two and went on to the checkered flag. This win claimed owner Little's first-ever victory in Madison, Indiana. It would not be his last.

The community-owned, MISS MADISON took first-place in Heat 1-B of the 1970 Madison Regatta. She dropped from contention when she stalled and restarted in the Final Heat and had to settle for a distant fifth.

MISS OWENSBORO

The next year would be a different story.

Precious little can be said of the fabulous 1971 Madison Regatta that hasn't already been said. The city's 60th boat racing anniversary story would amaze a fiction writer. Chapter Eight will recall in detail this exceptional race day.

The MISS MADISON of 1971 represented the end of an era. She was the last Unlimited hydroplane with the old-style rear cockpit, forward engine, shovel-nosed bow configuration to ever achieve victory.

To prove that the hometown performance was anything but a fluke, MISS MADISON captured first-place honors in the Tri-Cities Atomic Cup three weeks later on the Columbia River at Kennewick, Washington.

A World Championship Race, sanctioned by the Union of International Motorboating in Brussels, Belgium, was the headline event for the 1972 Madison Regatta, which unlike the previous year was plagued with more problems than a math book.

The flood-swollen-debris-filled Ohio River very nearly forced cancellation of the race, which was run on Independence Day instead of July 2 as originally scheduled.

Madison -- Hydroplane Heritage - Fred Farley & Ron Harsin

Qualifications had to be scrubbed and Referee Ken Wright declared the race a contest after two sets of elimination heats. No Final Heat was run. Impaired visibility and the renewed appearance of driftwood and debris stirred up by the unexpected appearance of the DELTA QUEEN as she plowed through the race course forced the cancellation.

Joe Schoenith's ATLAS VAN LINES easily won Heats 1-B and 2-B to claim that team's third Madison victory since 1954 and driver Bill Muncey's fourth since 1960. Terry Sterett finished runner-up for the second year in a row at Madison, this time with MISS BUDWEISER, which outdistanced third-place GO GALE with Tom Sheehy over the finish line by one tenth of a second in Heat 1-A.

The initial hometown appearance of a newly constructed MISS MADISON did not materialize at the 1972 Madison Regatta. The craft suffered extensive damage and sank the previous week at Detroit with rookie driver Charlie Dunn at the controls.

The Indiana Governor's Cup returned to the top of the shelf in 1973. It was won that year by Dave Heerensperger's new super-fast PAY 'n PAK, which utilized a horizontal stabilizer wing and was nicknamed the "Winged Wonder." Designed by Ron Jones, the 1973 PAY 'n PAK was wider and flatter than most of her contemporaries. It represented the next generation of hull design, which was to dominate Unlimited racing for the next several years.

Although not significantly faster on the straightaway than the other post-World War II Unlimited hydroplanes, the PAK could corner better and faster than any boat ever built to that time.

PAY 'n PAK with Mickey Remund driving re-wrote the record book at the 1973 Madison Regatta with a lap in qualification of 116.580 and a lap in competition of 112.080.

Remund and the PAK outperformed second-place Dean Chenoweth in MISS BUDWEISER and third-place

Danny Walls in LINCOLN THRIFT'S 7-1/4% SPECIAL.

Mickey experienced some anxious moments in the Final Heat when the PAY 'n PAK's aluminum steering wheel broke apart in his hands prior to the start when two of the three spokes of the wheel came loose. Remund managed to win by firmly gripping the one spoke and the base of the wheel in the hope that it would all hold together.

PAY 'n PAK
This boat would later become a MISS MADISON

The PAY 'n PAK team returned in 1974 with George Henley as driver. George duplicated Mickey's achievement of the year before with victories in all three heats. He also set another batch of local speed distinctions, which included a competition lap of 114.796.

Dean Chenoweth again occupied the runner-up spot with MISS BUDWEISER, while third-place in 1974 went to MISS MADISON with promising rookie driver Milner Irvin at the wheel. Irvin would see intermittent duty with the MISS MADISON team over the next decade.

The 1974 regatta was conducted in October after tornado damage in the spring of that year prompted cancellation of the traditional Fourth of July weekend date.

For pure boat racing, the 1975 Indiana Governor's Cup

ranks right up there with the greatest Unlimited races of all time. Seldom has the sport witnessed a more action-packed contest.

George Henley and the "Winged Wonder" PAY 'n PAK emerged victorious once again, but only after a titanic struggle.

Heat 2-A was an absolute classic when Henley and the PAK ran deck-to-deck with Billy Schumacher and the WEISFIELD'S for five heart-stopping laps. George outmaneuvered Billy over the finish line at a record-breaking 115.148 miles per hour to 115.060 for the 12-1/2-mile distance. It doesn't get much closer.

The 1975 racing season is remembered as the last hurrah for the old-style Thunderboats with their traditional World War II fighter aircraft engines. The once-plentiful supply of Allison and Rolls-Royce Merlin V-12 power plants was now badly depleted. In general, the late 1970s and early 1980s were not vintage years for Unlimited racing. Not until the turbine revolution of 1984 would the sport experience a renaissance.

The 1976 Madison Regatta was one of the more disappointing in the series. Only seven Unlimiteds assembled to compete for the Indiana Governor's Cup after a particularly destructive race the week before in Detroit. Two prominent contenders, the MISS BUDWEISER and the OLYMPIA BEER, had sunk and weren't available to run at Madison, although both teams were represented on the Ohio River by slower back-up hulls.

First-place in 1976, for an unprecedented fourth year in a row, was the phenomenal PAY 'n PAK hull, renamed ATLAS VAN LINES by its new owner/driver Bill Muncey in his fifth winning performance at Madison.

ATLAS and Muncey simply outclassed second-place Tom D'Eath and MISS U.S. ATLAS VAN LINES averaged 109.462 in the winner-take-all Final Heat, compared to

105.783 for MISS U.S.

MISS MADISON finished a solid third in 1976. Jockey, Ron Snyder brought the hometown crowd to its feet when he took first-place in Heat 2-A over Tom Sheehy and the substitute MISS BUDWEISER.

The 1977 season witnessed the debut of the fabulously successful ATLAS VAN LINES "Blue Blaster," owned and driven by Muncey. Co-designed by Jim Lucero and Dixon Smith, the "Blaster" became the first cabover (or forward-cockpit) hull to dominate in the Unlimited Class. ATLAS VAN LINES won six out of nine races in 1977 and seemed to be a shoo-in for the National High Point Championship. This was not to be because of the boat's incredibly poor showing at the Madison Regatta.

Muncey and ATLAS had a fourth and a "Did Not Finish" in the preliminary action and didn't qualify for the Final Heat. The VAN LINES gave up over 1000 points to Mickey Remund and the MISS BUDWEISER that day. This ultimately cost ATLAS VAN LINES the championship (by 904 points) at season's end.

MISS BUDWEISER owner, Bernie Little, ended a seven-year dryspell at Madison with a clear-cut victory in 1977. Remund and MISS BUD averaged 102.763 in the finale, followed by Tom Sheehy and ANHEUSER-BUSCH NATURAL LIGHT, also owned by Little, at 99.778. Then came third-place Ron Snyder in MISS NORTH TOOL, Jon Peddie in MISS MADISON and Bob Maschmedt in DIONYSES.

The ATLAS VAN LINES team of owner/driver Muncey and crew chief Lucero vindicated themselves in 1978 at Madison. They won the Indiana Governor's Cup hands-down with a speed of 109.489 in the Final Heat. No one else was even close. This was in spite of loosing the horizontal stabilizer in the first heat and suffering damage to the port side of the hull in a later heat.

Second-place in the 1978 Indiana Governor's Cup went to THE SQUIRE SHOP, owned by Bob Steil and driven by 24-year-old Lee "Chip" Hanauer. Chip was making his first appearance at Madison. Four years later, Hanauer would replace Muncey as ATLAS VAN LINES pilot after Bill was fatally injured in a "blow-over" accident with the "Blue Blaster" at Acapulco, Mexico, in 1981.

THE SQUIRE SHOP

The seventh and final victory by Bill Muncey at Madison, Indiana, occurred in 1979. He won in 1960 with MISS THRIFTWAY, in 1961-62 with MISS CENTURY 21 and in 1972-76-78-79 with ATLAS VAN LINES.

The 1979 Madison Regatta marked the town's 30th anniversary as a host for Unlimited hydroplane racing. This was a Gold Cup year and ten teams gathered to do competitive battle. These included a trio of new hulls: the Rolls-Royce Griffon-powered MISS BUDWEISER, designed by Ron Jones and a couple Merlin boats from the drawing board of Dave Knowlen, THE SQUIRE SHOP and the MISS CIRCUS CIRCUS.

The Ohio River was extremely rough on race day. Going into the first turn of the Final Heat, MISS CIRCUS CIRCUS and driver Steve Reynolds landed in a deep "hole." Reynolds was almost flipped out of the boat and his foot came off throttle. Steve restarted the engine and took off after the front-running ATLAS VAN LINES. Bill Muncey would not be denied his victory.

1979 MISS CIRCUS CIRCUS

At the finish line, it was ATLAS VAN LINES the winner, a full mile ahead of MISS CIRCUS CIRCUS, followed by Hanauer in THE SQUIRE SHOP.

This was Muncey's eighth victory since 1956 in the APBA Gold Cup. To many sports fans, Bill was to boat racing what Babe Ruth was to baseball and Red Grange was to football. Muncey was 50 years old in 1979 with 27 months to live.

Madison -- Hydroplane Heritage - Fred Farley & Ron Harsin

Indiana Governor's Cup Winners

YEAR	WINNING BOAT	WINNING DRIVER
2003	MISS BUDWEISER	DAVE VILLWOCK
2002	MISS E-LAM PLUS	NATE BROWN
2001	OH BOY OBERTO/MADISON	STEVEN DAVID
2000	MISS BUDWEISER	DAVE VILLWOCK
1999	MISS PICO	CHIP HANAUER
1998	MISS BUDWEISER	DAVE VILLWOCK
1997	MISS BUDWEISER	DAVE VILLWOCK
1996	SMOKIN' JOE'S	MARK TATE
1995	SMOKIN' JOE'S	MARK TATE
1994	MISS BUDWEISER	CHIP HANAUER
1993	MISS BUDWEISER	CHIP HANAUER
1992	MISS BUDWEISER	CHIP HANAUER
1991	AMERICAN SPIRIT	MARK EVANS
1990	MISS CIRCUS CIRCUS	CHIP HANAUER
1989	MISS BUDWEISER	JIM KROPFELD
1988	MR. PRINGLES	SCOTT PIERCE
1987	MISS BUDWEISER	JIM KROPFELD
1986	MILLER AMERICAN	CHIP HANAUER
1985	MISS 7-ELEVEN	STEVE REYNOLDS
1984	ATLAS VAN LINES	CHIP HANAUER
1983	MISS BUDWEISER	JIM KROPFELD
1982	THE SQUIRE SHOP	TOM D'EATH
1981	MISS BUDWEISER	DEAN CHENOWETH
1980	MISS BUDWEISER	DEAN CHENOWETH
1979	ATLAS VAN LINES	BILL MUNCEY
1978	ATLAS VAN LINES	BILL MUNCEY
1977	MISS BUDWEISER	MICKEY REMUND
1976	ATLAS VAN LINES	BILL MUNCEY
1975	PAY 'N PAK	GEORGE HENLEY
1974	PAY 'N PAK	GEORGE HENLEY
1973	PAY 'N PAK	MICKEY REMUND

Madison -- Hydroplane Heritage - Fred Farley & Ron Harsin

1972 ATLAS VAN LINES BILL MUNCEY
1971 MISS MADISON JIM McCORMICK
1970 MISS BUDWEISER DEAN CHENOWETH
1969 MYR'S SPECIAL DEAN CHENOWETH
1968 MISS BARDAHL BILLY SCHUMACHER
1967 MISS BARDAHL BILLY SCHUMACHER
1966 TAHOE MISS MIRA SLOVAK
1965 TAHOE MISS CHUCK THOMPSON
1964 TAHOE MISS CHUCK THOMPSON
1963 MISS EXIDE BILL BROW
1962 MISS CENTURY 21 BILL MUNCEY
1961 MISS CENTURY 21 BILL MUNCEY
1960 MISS THRIFTWAY BILL MUNCEY
1959 HAWAII KAI III RON MUSSON
1958 MISS U.S. I DON WILSON
1957 HAWAII KAI III JACK REGAS
1956 MISS U.S. I FRED ALTER
1955 TEMPO VII DANNY FOSTER
1954 GALE IV BILL CANTRELL
1953 WILDCATTER BURNETT BARTLEY, JR.
1952 WILDCATTER BURNETT BARTLEY, JR.
1951 HORNET MARION COOPER
FIRST RACE: 1911

Kristen Johnson - Miss Madison Regatta - 2002 holds the Indiana Govenor's Cup.

Madison -- Hydroplane Heritage - Fred Farley & Ron Harsin

Chapter Six
History of MISS MADISON

Please note that over the years, six boats have raced with the MISS MADISON name. The sixth MISS MADISON was actually a rental. When the new MISS MADISON crashed at San Diego in 1988, the MISS MADISON team leased the U-3 RISLEY'S hull from owners Ed Cooper, Sr. and Ed Cooper, Jr., for the final race of the year in Las Vegas. The U-3 was, officially, the U-6 MISS MADISON at this one event.

*U-6 MISS MADISON (lst) ***
1961 - 1963
* Formerly U-79 NITROGEN was donated to the town of Madison, Indiana by Samuel DuPont.

Madison -- Hydroplane Heritage - Fred Farley & Ron Harsin

U-6 MISS MADISON (2nd) **
1963 - 1971
** Formerly U-79-2 NITROGEN TOO
The 1971 Gold Cup Champion
When the first MISS MADISON was destroyed, this second MISS MADISON was purchased from Samuel DuPont for a price of $5000.

U-6 MISS MADISON (3rd)
1972 - 1977

Madison -- Hydroplane Heritage - Fred Farley & Ron Harsin

U-6 MISS MADISON (4th) ***
1978 - 1988
*** *Formerly U-25 (and U-1) PAY 'n PAK and U-76 ATLAS VAN LINES.*

As the MISS MADISON, this boat also ran with the sponsor names AMERICAN SPEEDY PRINTING, HOLSET MISS MADISON and MISS RICH PLAN MOBILE FOOD SERVICE

U-6 MISS MADISON (5th)
1988 - 2003
This hydroplane started it's career with an Allison Engine. The boat also ran as the HOLSET MISS MADISON.

Madison -- Hydroplane Heritage - Fred Farley & Ron Harsin

U-6 MISS MADISON (5th)

Note that the same (5th) MISS MADISON has been upgraded to run a Turbine Engine.

Madison -- Hydroplane Heritage - Fred Farley & Ron Harsin

This is the same MISS MADISON hull. However, bringing in a sponsor allowed the boat to continue operations. This boat ran with several sponsors such as: Holset, Dewalt Tools, Kelloggs Sugar Frosted Flakes, Jasper Engines and Oh Boy! Oberto Beef Snacks. Several of these sponsored boats are shown over the next few pages. These are all MISS MADISON boats painted for the sponsor company.

Madison -- Hydroplane Heritage - Fred Farley & Ron Harsin

Madison -- Hydroplane Heritage - Fred Farley & Ron Harsin

VALVOLINE\HOLSET MISS MADISON

Other MISS MADISON sponsors have included Nestea Ice Tea, Hardee's, Holset Miss Mazda, Dr. Toyota, Hamms Bear (yes, Bear is correct, not beer) and Barney Armstrong's Machine.

Madison -- Hydroplane Heritage - Fred Farley & Ron Harsin

The current (5th) MISS MADISON sponsored by Oh Boy! Oberto Beef Snacks.

MISS MADISON (6th)

Very few individuals know that a 6th boat carried the MISS MADISON name. To keep the standings in the National Points race, the RISLEY'S was RENTED and ran as the MISS MADISON in one race while repairs were being made to the damaged original.

Madison -- Hydroplane Heritage - Fred Farley & Ron Harsin

MISS MADISON Power Plants

Allison V-12 - 1961 - 1990

Lycoming Turbine - 1991 - present

Drivers of the MISS MADISON

Marion Cooper - The First Driver of the MISS MADISON

The community-owned, MISS MADISON from southern Indiana has competed for more consecutive seasons than any other Unlimited hydroplane team. Forty-three years, starting in 1961.

The original MISS MADISON was a gift to the city by industrialist Samuel F. DuPont of Wilmington, Delaware. DuPont had raced the hull during 1958, 1959 and 1960 as the NITROGEN with Bob Hayward, Fred Alter, Don Dunnington and Norm Evans as drivers.

When NITROGEN assumed the MISS MADISON identity, Graham Heath of Madison became the crew chief and Marion Cooper of Louisville, Kentucky, was appointed as driver.

Cooper had been racing boats since the 1930s. He had been the back-up driver for SLO-MO-SHUN IV and SLO-MO-SHUN V in 1955 and had handled MISS ROCKET in the 1957 Gold Cup at Seattle.

In a 1973 interview with Fred Farley, Marion recalled his tenure as the original MISS MADISON pilot.

"I had often driven for Neal Cahall and Dick Cox in the 225s and 266s. They were involved in the MISS MADISON organization when Sam DuPont gave them the first boat. They called me and wanted to know if I'd drive it and, of course, I was happy to do so."

"During the first year, they didn't have another stock Allison, so the same engine was run the entire season. We tried to hold the RPMs down to around 4000 or 4100.

If it went above that, it was only for a short time. We didn't figure it would run very long above that."

"At the end of the season, since the Madison Regatta was the last race, the organization said I could let it go, so I did and took fourth in an eleven-boat field."

Marion Cooper and the Original Miss Madison Crew

During his two seasons as MISS MADISON's pilot, Cooper also took fifth in both the 1961 Detroit Memorial Regatta and the 1961 President's Cup, sixth in the 1962 Gold Cup, fourth in the 1962 Spirit Of Detroit Trophy and third in the 1962 Madison Regatta.

Marion finished every heat in which he started with MISS MADISON and scored points in all but two.

Cooper's most memorable race with MISS MADISON occurred on the warm, sunny afternoon of August 5, 1961, during the Seafair Regatta on Lake Washington. Three races of 45 miles in length were run that day for fast, middle and slow qualifiers. MISS MADISON triumphed in the intermediate race for the Seattle Trophy with heat speeds of 99.046, 98.937 and 100.074. Each heat was five laps around a 3-mile course.

"In the First Heat, I got up to the starting line a little too early and had to back off. By the time I got on it again, the others had all gone by me. I stayed back there in all that rough water until about the last lap when I went by two of the three boats ahead of me on the outside and took second-place points.

"In the next two heats, I got good starts and won both of them. In the Second Heat, the exhaust stack broke off on the right side and was firing into the hull, which finally started to blaze. Then a three-quarter inch water plug on the right bank blew out. The water from that plug started hitting the fire and putting it out. The resulting steam was flying about seven or eight feet in the air. I think everybody thought the engine was cooking, but it wasn't. I watched the temperature gauge, but the water from the plug kept the fire down until we finished. Of course, for the Final Heat, they put another exhaust stack on and another plug in it and everything was all right again."

"The memory of that race is especially fond, due to the enormous crowd and because the race in Seattle was a big deal, more so than anyplace else in the country."

Following his retirement from competition, Cooper remained a familiar and popular boat racing figure. He always attended the annual Madison Regatta until his death in 1986.

The MISS MADISON organization called upon Marion to "break in" new drivers for the team. When George "Buddy" Byers was named pilot in 1963, Cooper took the boat out, checked the systems and then turned the wheel over to Buddy. Marion did the same thing three years later when rookie Jim McCormick became driver of MISS MADISON.

In counseling new drivers just starting out, Cooper believed that "If a rookie can get into an Unlimited, then that's the thing to do. He could learn to drive in it just as easy as he could starting in a Limited. That's because they drive entirely different. Of course, that doesn't happen very often, but it does happen occasionally. And I'd say he would be as good a driver as one who started small and then worked his way up."

"The two hard points about driving an Unlimited are in going way back at the start and in keeping the transom up, going around the turns. Running a three-to-one gear ratio, if you let it drop, you may as well forget about it."

When asked about the changes he had observed in the sport since his departure from it, Marion was one of the first to recognize the potential of the horizontal stabilizer wing that the Ron Jones-designed PAY 'n PAK introduced in 1973: "You'll see more of those lift wings stuck on the back ends of more boats. They're a big help in getting around a corner."

Cooper saw no future in the repeated attempts at twin-automotive power in the APBA Unlimited Class.

On the subject of the great drivers of the past and present, Marion felt it was, as he stated, "pretty much of a draw. Bill Cantrell was rough. But of the new ones, I would just as soon risk Dean Chenoweth with a boat as any at all."

Cooper will always be remembered as being the first in a long and distinguished line of MISS MADISON drivers over the past four decades.

Following in Marion's footsteps are Buddy Byers, Jim McCormick, Morlan Visel, Ed O'Halloran, Charlie Dunn, Tom Sheehy, Milner Irvin, Jerry Bangs, Ron Snyder, Jon Peddie, Andy Coker, Jerry Hopp, Mitch Evans, Mike Hanson, Todd Yarling, Charley Wiggins, Nate Brown and Steve David.

MISS MADISON Drivers

Marion Cooper
1961, 1962

A boat racer since the 1930s, Marion Cooper piloted MISS MADISON to its first victory. This was the secondary race for the Seattle Trophy at the 1961 World's Championship Seafair Regatta. Due to budgetary constraints, Cooper had to make due with a single Allison engine in 1961 and had to make it last all year. Prior to handling MISS MADISON Marion piloted HERMES III, MERCURY, MISS ROCKET and was a back-up driver for SLO-MO-SHUN IV and SLO-MO-SHUN V.

Morlan Visel
1963

Morlan Visel had a very brief assignment as MISS MADISON's driver. It ended tragically. Called on to replace the retiring Marion Cooper at the 1963 APBA Gold Cup, Visel was badly injured in a test run when the boat struck floating debris and was destroyed. Morlan raced Limited hydroplanes in the 1940s. He owned and drove two Unlimiteds prior to MISS MADISON. These were HURRICANE IV between 1948 and 1953 and HURRICANE VI in 1962.

George "Buddy" Byers
1963, 1964, 1965

One of the top 7-Litre Limited drivers of the 1950s, Buddy Byers achieved the Unlimited level in 1963 with the second MISS MADISON. He piloted MISS MADISON to second-place in National High Points in 1964 and scored the first major victory for the MISS MADISON team. This was the 1965 Dixie Cup at Guntersville, Alabama. Signed to drive Bill Harrah's TAHOE MISS in 1966, Byers was injured in a Limited hydroplane accident at Miami Marine Stadium and retired from racing.

"Gentleman" Jim McCormick
1966, 1969, 1970, 1971

The only driver to score back-to-back victories with MISS MADISON (the 1971 APBA Gold Cup and Atomic Cup races), Jim McCormick first served notice of his competitive prowess when he won the 266 Cubic Inch Class race at the 1964 Madison Regatta with MISS KATHLEEN. In addition to MISS MADISON McCormick also piloted NOTRE DAME, WAYFARERS CLUB LADY, ATLAS VAN LINES, HARRAH'S CLUB, MISS TIMEX, RED MAN, PAY 'n PAK and SANTA RITA HOMES in the Unlimited Class.

Ed O'Halloran
1967, 1968

During Jim McCormick's two-year absence from the cockpit of MISS MADISON in the late 1960s, Ed O'Halloran was driver of MISS MADISON. A Detroit area Limited competitor, O'Halloran debuted in the Unlimited Class in 1964 with Mike Wolfbauer's SAVAIR'S MIST. He also piloted SUCH CRUST IV, MY GYPSY and MY CUPIEE. In his first appearance at the wheel of the community-owned U-6, Ed finished second in the 1967 Tampa Suncoast Cup with a victory in Heat One.

Charlie Dunn
1972, 1973

The first driver of the third MISS MADISON, which debuted in 1972, Charlie Dunn joined the community-owned U-6 team on the strength of his performance in the 5-Litre "F" Class. As driver of MISS WASHINGTON, D.C., "Chargin' Charlie" won an incredible 84 heats in a row. Dunn did not enjoy the same success with Unlimited hydroplanes. After a third-place finish with MISS MADISON at the 1972 Owensboro (Kentucky) Regatta, Charlie crashed MISS MADISON to the bottom the Detroit River during qualification for the 1972 Gold Cup.

Tom Sheehy
1973, 1982

The 1971 Unlimited Rookie-of-the Year with MISS TIMEX, Tom Sheehy, got the chance to drive the third MISS MADISON when Charlie Dunn resigned in mid-season 1973. Sheehy also piloted another MISS MADISON briefly in 1982. His best finish with the U-6 team was a second-place in the 1982 "Thunder In The Park" at Geneva, New York. Tom also saw action with GO GALE, RED MAN, MISS TECHNICOLOR, SUNNY JIM and ANHEUSER-BUSCH NATURAL LIGHT during his career.

E. Milner Irvin III
1974, 1978, 1979, 1980, 1981, 1984

A last-minute addition to the 1974 MISS MADISON team (when Tom Sheehy departed to accept another assignment), Milner Irvin qualified as an Unlimited driver at Miami...and nearly won the race. He finished third overall and defeated the winners, Howie Benns and MISS BUDWEISER, in the Final Heat. In 1981 at Acapulco, Mexico, Irvin risked his own life when he spun MISS MADISON at high speed to avoid running over the fatally injured Bill Muncey, driver of ATLAS VAN LINES.

Jerry Bangs
1975

A trial lawyer by profession and a hydroplane racer by avocation, Jerry Bangs brought a lot of class to Unlimited racing. In ten races as pilot of MISS MADISON (also known as HAMM'S BEAR), Bangs qualified for the all-important Final Heat six times in 1975 and finished fifth in National High Points. Jerry was fatally injured two years later, as driver of SQUIRE, when he was thrown out of the boat at the Seattle Seafair Regatta on Lake Washington.

Madison -- Hydroplane Heritage - Fred Farley & Ron Harsin

Ron Snyder
1976, 1982, 1983, 1984, 1986, 1987, 1988

The only driver to pilot three different MISS MADISON hulls in competition. Ron Snyder guided the U-6 to a total of 15 podium finishes (first, second, or third). These included his 1983 victory in the Missouri Governor's Cup at Lake-of-the-Ozarks with MISS MADISON (alias MISS RICH PLAN). Snyder also drove MISS BUDWEISER and the Madison-based MISS KENTUCKIANA PAVING during his career. Ron survived a spectacular "blow-over" accident with MISS MADISON at San Diego in 1988. He credited the recently mandated F-16 safety canopy with saving his life.

Madison -- Hydroplane Heritage - Fred Farley & Ron Harsin

Jon Peddie
1977, 1978

A veteran auto racer, Jon Peddie had never driven a hydroplane in his life when signed to pilot MISS MADISON in 1977. Jon readied himself for the assignment by test-driving Denny Jackson's RIDE-ON, a 280 Cubic Inch Class hydro. Peddie piloted MISS MADISON to fourth-place in a field of 20 boats in 1977 National High Points and was honored as Unlimited Rookie-of-the-Year. In 1978, Jon took second-place with MISS MADISON in the APBA Gold Cup at Owensboro, Kentucky, with a victory in Heat-3. Peddie also finished third in the 1982 Madison Regatta as driver of MISS KENTUCKIANA PAVING.

Andy Coker
1985, 1986

When Ron Snyder took a one-year leave-of-absence from MISS MADISON in 1985 Andy Coker took his place. Coker had been racing boats since 1958, starting with the APBA Stock Outboard division. He was also a record-setting 5-Litre Inboard competitor. As pilot of MISS MADISON Andy won Unlimited Rookie-of-the-Year honors and finished second in the races at Miami and Syracuse. Coker returned to the cockpit of MISS MADISON for one event in 1986 and finished fifth in the Tri-Cities (Washington) Columbia Cup.

Jerry Hopp
1986, & 2000

Sooner or later, every Unlimited hydroplane team needs the services of a relief driver when the regular pilot is injured or unavailable. Three times in its history, the MISS MADISON team has called upon veteran racer Jerry Hopp to fill in behind the wheel of MISS MADISON. Twice in 1986, Hopp substituted for Ron Snyder at Evansville and Philadelphia. In 2000, he relieved Charley Wiggins at Detroit when Jerry had about 15 minutes notice before stepping into MISS MADISON -- a boat he had never driven. Hopp went on to take fifth in the Gold Cup.

Mike Hanson
*1988, 1989, 1990, 1991, 1992, 1993, 1994, 1995,
1996, 1997, 1998*

In his first appearance as MISS MADISON's driver, Mike Hanson was run over by another boat (MISS CIRCUS CIRCUS), while returning to the pits after one of the heats of the 1988 Seattle Seafair Regatta. From that rather abrupt beginning, things could only get better and they did. For the next ten years, Hanson served as both driver and hull specialist for the U-6 team. He finished third in National High Points in 1989 and second in 1993. Mike won the Star Mart Cup with MISS MADISON (alias KELLOGG'S FROSTED FLAKES) in 1993.

Mitch Evans
1988

Most people are surprised to see Mitch Evans included on the honor roll of MISS MADISON (U-6) drivers. The circumstances are unusual. In 1988, the new Ron Jones-designed MISS MADISON was badly damaged in a "blow-over" accident at San Diego. In order to fulfill a sponsorship agreement with Holset Engineering, the City of Madison leased Ed Cooper's RISLEY'S (U-3) hydroplane for the Silver Cup race on Lake Mead the following weekend. The U-3 became the U-6 for that one event. Evans, who regularly drove for the Cooper team, piloted the substitute MISS MADISON to fifth-place.

Todd Yarling
1999

A graduate of the 280 Cubic Inch Class Inboard wars, Todd Yarling advanced to the Unlimited ranks in 1983 as pilot of Jim Sedam's MISS TOSTI ASTI (U-22). He finished third in his debut race at Lake-of-the-Ozarks, Missouri and was named Rookie-of-the-Year. A resident of Hanover, Indiana, Yarling had handled no fewer than eight Unlimited hydroplanes prior to his 1999 appointment as MISS MADISON driver. He flipped MISS MADISON in a race at Barrie, Ontario, but rebounded to take third in the Virginia Is For Lovers Cup at Norfolk, Virginia.

Madison -- Hydroplane Heritage - Fred Farley & Ron Harsin

Charley Wiggins
2000

A promising Limited competitor from Gadsden, Alabama, Charley Wiggins had a painfully short tenure as driver of MISS MADISON. He joined the U-6 team on the strength of his stellar performance in the Unlimited Light Racing Series. Wiggins had in fact won the ULRS race at the 1995 Madison Regatta aboard HIGH PRESSURE. Charley finished sixth with MISS MADISON in the 2000 Indiana Governor's Cup, but after suffering injuries at both Evansville and Detroit, he retired from racing.

Nate Brown
2000

Following the retirement of Charley Wiggins as MISS MADISON pilot in mid-season 2000, veteran Unlimited competitor Nate Brown was hired to drive at the three western races. Under the sponsorship of OH BOY! OBERTO, Brown qualified for all three Final Heats. He was third at the Tri-Cities, fourth at Seattle and third at San Diego. Following his successful U-6 stint, Nate went to work for MISS E-LAM PLUS (U-16). Brown won four races with the U-16 in 2001 and 2002, including the 2002 Indiana Governor's Cup at Madison.

Steve David
2001, 2002, 2003

Unlimited hydroplane fans caught their first glimpse of Steve David when he was Rookie-of-the-Year in 1988 with POCKET SAVERS PLUS (U-4), co-owned by Jim McCormick and Bob Fendler. Steve had a long and successful career with the Jim Harvey Motorsports team throughout the 1990s but retired mid-way through the 1999 season. Nevertheless, the siren call of Unlimited racing was too great to resist. In 2001, David returned to score a popular victory with MISS MADISON as OH BOY! OBERTO in the Madison Regatta.

MISS MADISON Race Victories

(1) 1965 - DIXIE CUP, Guntersville, AL
Driver - Buddy Byers
(2) 1971 - APBA GOLD CUP
INDIANA GOVERNOR'S CUP, Madison, IN
Driver - Jim McCormick
(3) 1971 - ATOMIC CUP, Tri-Cities, WA
Driver - Jim McCormick
(4) 1983 - MISSOURI GOVERNOR'S CUP
Lake Ozark, MO
Driver - Ron Snyder
(5) 1993 - STAR MART CUP, San Diego, CA
Driver - Mike Hanson
(6) 2001 - INDIANA GOVERNOR'S CUP
Madison, IN
Driver - Steve David

TWO UNUSUAL VICTORIES BY MISS MADISON

Two of MISS MADISON's more unusual victories were the 1983 Missouri Governor's Cup at Lake-of-the-Ozarks and the 1993 Star Mart Cup on San Diego's Mission Bay. In both instances, MISS MADISON was considered a long-shot at best.

At Lake-of-the-Ozarks, MISS MADISON (racing as MISS RICH PLAN) had to make do with an obsolete hull. The boat was ten years old and not in the same design genre as

ATLAS VAN LINES or MISS BUDWEISER, the two top-rated teams, which had state-of-the-art hulls.

As the final seconds ticked away prior to the start of the Final Heat, ATLAS driver Chip Hanauer and MISS BUD pilot Jim Kropfeld were so worried about each other that they mistimed their starts badly. They crossed the starting line dead last.

MISS MADISON's Ron Snyder, a master of the clock start, timed his approach to the starting line perfectly. Snyder led from wire-to-wire, while an embarrassed Hanauer and Kropfeld played a hopeless game of catch-up.

At the finish line, Snyder had a clear lead. He claimed the first race victory in twelve years for the city of Madison. Ron proved that an important element of racing is being in the right place at the right time when opportunity knocks.

A decade later, at San Diego, MISS MADISON, campaigning as KELLOGG'S FROSTED FLAKES, was having a miserable day. Mechanical difficulties plagued driver Mike Hanson who was unable to score points in any of his preliminary heats.

MISS MADISON advanced to the Final Heat on the basis of having finished first in the Last Chance Heat. This only entitled Hanson to start from the "trailer-boat" position, outside and well behind the other finalists.

The trailer-boat spot is the worst position on the race course. Never in the history of Unlimited racing had any boat ever won from the trailer-boat position, but that's exactly what happened at San Diego in 1993.

Hanson worked his way up through the field, through the battering wakes of the other boats. Mike passed one entry and then another...and another...and another. After five laps, MISS MADISON was in the lead, taking the checkered flag.

"I felt we had no chance to win," proclaimed a jubilant Hanson, "but I proved myself wrong."

Madison -- Hydroplane Heritage - Fred Farley & Ron Harsin

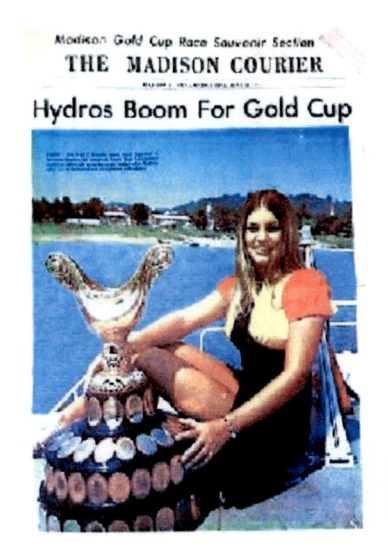

1971 Regatta Queen, Carol Eggman, with the Gold Cup (left)
2002 Regatta Queen, Kristen Johnson, with the Indiana Governor's Cup (right)

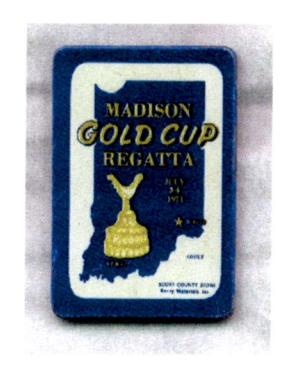

1971 adult admission badge (left)
1971 limited edition MISS MADISON Crew Member badge

Color Insert - 1

Madison -- Hydroplane Heritage - Fred Farley & Ron Harsin

MISS MADISON takes the lead in the 1971 Gold Cup Race

1971 MISS MADISON Gold Cup Winner

Madison -- Hydroplane Heritage - Fred Farley & Ron Harsin

Jim McCormick comes in after winning the 1971 Gold Cup

Valvoline MISS MADISON

Madison -- Hydroplane Heritage - Fred Farley & Ron Harsin

Tony The Tiger MISS MADISON

DeWalt Tools MISS MADISON

Color Insert - 4

Madison -- Hydroplane Heritage - Fred Farley & Ron Harsin

Oh Boy! Oberto MISS MADISON
2001 Indiana Governor's Cup winner

Vintage boats running at Madison, Indiana

Madison -- Hydroplane Heritage - Fred Farley & Ron Harsin

W D RACING, Limited Hydroplane

CLOSE SHAVE - Limited Hydroplane

Madison -- Hydroplane Heritage - Fred Farley & Ron Harsin

HINKLE'S, Limited Hydroplane

RIDE ON, Limited Hydroplane

Madison -- Hydroplane Heritage - Fred Farley & Ron Harsin

MISS BUDWIESER flips during a race

1991 MISS BUDWIESER

Madison -- Hydroplane Heritage - Fred Farley & Ron Harsin

MISS BUDWIESER as it appeared in the movie Madison with the driver in the front seat and the actor in the rear seat.

The only known color photograph of the BILL-DER

Madison -- Hydroplane Heritage - Fred Farley & Ron Harsin

Bill Muncey in the BLUE BLASTER (Atlas)

Nate Brown flying U-16, MISS E-LAM PLUS

Mark Evans driving U-8, LUMAR WINDOW FILM

Madison -- Hydroplane Heritage - Fred Farley & Ron Harsin

U-10, MISS EMCOR catching too much air.

MISS BUD, OH BOY! OBERTO & MISS EMCOR

Mike Hanson driving TUBBY'S SUBMARINE SANDWICHES

Madison -- Hydroplane Heritage - Fred Farley & Ron Harsin

U-10, MISS EMCOR

CELLULAR ONE after losing a sponson

Madison -- Hydroplane Heritage - Fred Farley & Ron Harsin

Chapter Seven
Madison The Movie

THE MADISON COURIER

WHEN HOLLYWOOD MEETS MADISON

Young Jake Lloyd, who starred in "Star Wars Episode One - The Phantom Menace," got to feel and hear the sights and sounds of the Madison Regatta Friday on the riverfront. Jake, who served as grand marshal of the regatta parade, covered his ears as a boat roared by during an afternoon practice. For a complete look at Friday's regatta qualifying and a preview of the weekend's racing see today's sports pages.

STAFF PHOTO BY JAMES V. CARROLL

While the turbine hydroplanes of today's racing circuit were taking to the water for the 1999 Madison, Indiana Governors Cup race, a film crew was setting up along the banks of the Ohio River to film a major motion picture. The film crew had old, vintage hydroplanes taken out of barns and museums, repainted, engines repaired and were ready to recreate the 1971 Madison Gold Cup Race.

Between heats of the 1999 race, the vintage boats took to the water and the cameras started filming. The film crew and vintage boats traveled across the nation to film other annual hydroplane races. Thousands of Madison residents volunteered to be extras in the movie. The little town of Madison, Indiana became center stage for a movie that will be shown in theaters across America and around the world.

Over the next several pages, we provide a look at how the movie was made. Please keep in mind, this book's major focus is about the actual events that took place in the 1971 race.

Movie Review

The movie MADISON, directed by William Bindley, should do for boat racing what John Frankenheimer's 1966 film GRAND PRIX did for car racing. MADISON is a magnificent calling card for the sport in general and the city of Madison, Indiana, in particular.

MADISON had its Mid-West premiere on Thursday, October 18, 2001, at the Heartland Film Festival in Indianapolis. The capacity crowd, which included a large delegation from the tiny Ohio River town, gave the film a standing ovation at the end of the screening.

The racing sequences were stunningly photographed. On the big screen, they were simply breathtaking. MADISON is a movie that demands to be seen in a theatre -- not on television. The camera pays loving attention to the picturesque southern Indiana locations.

The script is based on the true story of the underdog MISS MADISON Unlimited hydroplane, which won the 1971 APBA Gold Cup with Jim McCormick driving.

Madison -- Hydroplane Heritage - *Fred Farley & Ron Harsin*

Strictly speaking, MADISON is not a racing film. It is the story of a man and his son -- Jim and Mike McCormick -- and the effect racing has on an economically challenged community. Actors, Jim Caviezel as Jim and Jake Lloyd as Mike, bring their characters to life. Hollywood legend Bruce Dern does a memorable star turn as Harry Volpi, whose prowess with the Allison engine proves invaluable to the MISS MADISON team.

Broadcaster Jim Hendrick, who announced the 1971 Gold Cup three decades ago, has a supporting role in the film as himself.

Some matters of historical fact are glossed over for dramatic effect. But this is a movie not a documentary, and as a movie, it succeeds on its own terms. Most importantly, the characters ring true. I knew all of the real people portrayed in the script and can visualize the real people saying and doing many of the things they say and do in the movie.

The sub-plot involving Jim McCormick's relationship with a young driver, played by actor Richard Lee Jackson, is an obvious reference to McCormick's real life friendship with George "Skipp" Walther. Skipp was fatally injured at Miami Marine Stadium in 1974 while testing the RED MAN hydroplane, which McCormick owned.

The film footage that represents the crash involving Jackson's character (fictionalized as "Buddy Johnson") is actually taken from KING-TV film of the 1962 MISS SEATTLE TOO disintegration on Seattle's, Lake Washington. The MISS SEATTLE TOO driver survived the boat's disintegration.

Power boat racing has definitely been given short shrift as a topic for Hollywood films. I've only seen two others and neither of these had to do with the Unlimited Class of hydroplane. One was CLAMBAKE, a mediocre Elvis vehicle, which did the sport no great service. The other was RACING FEVER, an absolutely wretched, drive-in opus from the early

'60s that makes PLAN 9 FROM OUTER SPACE look like GONE WITH THE WIND.

The MADISON movie is in a class by itself. Never has this much talent been lavished on a boat racing subject.

I've been a film buff almost as long as I have been a hydroplane fan. With MADISON, I'm able to enjoy both of my passions. When I read the script four years ago, I concluded that if the filmmakers adhered to the screenplay as written, they would have a pretty darned good movie. They did not disappoint me.

The first race I watched on the Ohio River was the 1971 Gold Cup. In my entire life, I've never been happier than when MISS MADISON flashed over the finish line as the winner. It was also the first race I attended that was won by a personal friend, Jim McCormick.

It was Jim's dream that this movie be made. Prior to his death in 1995, he had planned to portray his own father in an earlier version of the script.

When the end credits rolled during the screening in Indianapolis, I was pleased to see a montage of outtakes from the ABC WIDE WORLD OF SPORTS telecast incorporated into the film. Through the magic of motion pictures, my friend Jim was able to appear in "his" movie after all.

The Movie Cast

William Bindley
Director, Producer and Screenwriter for "Madison"
Other Credits:
Director
- The Eighteenth Angel (1997)
- Johnny & Clyde (1995)
- Judicial Consent (1994)

Scott Bindley
Screenwriter for "Madison"

Actors / Actresses

James Caviezel
Plays "Jim McCormick" in "Madison"
Other Credits:
The Count of Monte Cristo (2002)
- High Crimes (2002)
- Angel Eyes (2001)
- Frequency (2000)
- Pay It Forward (2000)
- Any Given Sunday (1999)
- Ride with the Devil (1999)
- The Thin Red Line (1998)
- G.I. Jane (1997)

Mary McCormack
Plays "Bonnie McCormick" in "Madison"
Other Credits:
Full Frontal (2002)
- World Traveler (2002)
- High Heels and Low Lifes (2001)
- K-Pax (2001)

- The Big Tease (2000)
- The Broken Hearts Club (2000)
- Gun Shy (2000)
- Other Voices (2000)
- Cash Crop (1999)
- Getting to Know You (1999)
- Mystery, Alaska (1999)
- True Crime (1999)
- Alarmist (1998)
- Private Parts (1997)
- Back Fire. (1994)

Jake Lloyd (right)
Note: He is autographing his "Star Wars - Anakin Skywalker" picture on the Pepsi bottle.

Jake Lloyd
Plays "Mike McCormick" in "Madison"
Other Credits:
Star Wars: Episode I - The Phantom Menace (1999)
 - Jingle All the Way (1996)
 - Unhook the Stars (1997)

Madison -- Hydroplane Heritage - Fred Farley & Ron Harsin

Bruce Dern
Plays "Harry Volpi" in "Madison"
Other Credits:
Into The Badlands/Rough Night in Jericho - 2 Pack (2002)
- The Glass House (2001)
- All the Pretty Horses (2000)
- John Wayne Collection (2000)
- One Last Score (1999)
- When the Bough Breaks II: Perfect Prey (1998)
- Small Soldiers (1998)
- Down Periscope (1996)
- Last Man Standing (1996)
- A Mother's Prayer (1995)
- Mrs. Munck (1995)
- Wild Bill (1995)
- Carolina Skeletons (1992)
- Diggstown (1992)
- After Dark, My Sweet (1990)
- The Court Martial of Jackie Robinson (1990)
- The Burbs (1989)
- 1969 (1988)
- World Gone Wild (1988)
- The Big Town (1987)
- Uncle Tom's Cabin (1987)
- On the Edge (1986)
- Toughlove (1985)
- Harry Tracy (1983)
- That Championship Season (1982)
- Tattoo (1981)
- Middle Age Crazy (1980)
- Coming Home (1978)
- The Driver (1978)
- Black Sunday (1976)
- Family Plot (1976)
- Posse (1975)

- Smile (1975)
- The Twist (1975)
- The Great Gatsby (1974)
- The Laughing Policeman (1973)
- The Cowboys (1972)
- The King of Marvin Gardens (1972)
- Thumb Tripping (1972)
- The Incredible Two-Headed Transplant (1971)
- Silent Running (1971)
- Cycle Savages, The (1969)
- Support Your Local Sheriff (1969)
- They Shoot Horses, Don't They? (1969)
- Psycho-Out (1968)
- Will Penny (1968)
- Rebel Rousers (1967)
- The Trip (1967)
- Waterhole #3 (1967)
- The Wild Angels (1966)
- Hush...Hush, Sweet Charlotte (1965)
- Marnie (1964)

Voice
- Small Soldiers (1998)

Brent Briscoe
Plays "Tony Steinhardt" in "Madison"
Other Credits::
Waking Up in Reno (2002)
- Double Take (2001)
- The Majestic (2001)
- Mulholland Drive (2001)
- Beautiful (2000)
- Another Day in Paradise (1998)
- A Simple Plan (1998)

Screenwriter
- Waking Up in Reno (2002)

Paul Dooley

Plays Mayor "Donald Vaughn" in "Madison"
Other Credits:
Insomnia (2002)
- Mad About You (2002)
- Guinevere (1999)
- Happy, Texas (1999)
- Runaway Bride (1999)
- Clockwatchers (1998)
- Angels in the End Zone (1997)
- Telling Lies In America (1997)
- Waiting for Guffman (1997)
- God's Lonely Man (1996)
- Out There (1995)
- Evolver (1994)
- The Underneath (1994)
- State of Emergency (1993)
- Shakes the Clown (1992)
- White Hot - The Mysterious Murder of Thelma Todd (1991)
- Flashback (1990)
- Last Rites (1988)
- Lip Service (1988)
- Monster in the Closet (1986)
- O.C. & Stiggs (1985)
- Sixteen Candles (1984)
- Strange Brew (1983)
- Endangered Species (1982)
- Kiss Me Goodbye (1982)
- Popeye (1980)
- Breaking Away (1979)
- Rich Kids (1979)
- A Wedding (1978)
- Foreplay (1974)

Richard Lee Jackson
Plays "Buddy" in "Madison"
Other Credits::
- Double Play (1997)

Cody McMains
Plays "Bobby Epperson" in "Madison"
Other Credits:
Not Another Teen Movie (2001)
- Bring It On (2000)
- Thomas and the Magic Railroad (2000)
- Tumbleweeds (1999)
- Big Bully (1996)
Voice
- Thomas and the Magic Railroad (2000)

Mark Fauser
Plays "Travis" in "Madison"
Other Credits:
Screenwriter
- Waking Up in Reno (2002)

Matthew Letscher
Plays "Owen Henderson" in "Madison"
Other Credits:
- The Mask of Zorro (1998)

Byrne Piven
Plays "George Wallin" in "Madison"
Other Credits:
- Wavelength (1995)

Madison -- Hydroplane Heritage - Fred Farley & Ron Harsin

Chelcie Ross
Plays "Roger Epperson" in "Madison"
Other Credits:
The Gift (2001)
• Novocaine (2001)
• Charming Billy (1998)
• A Simple Plan (1998)
• Evil Has a Face (1996)

William Shockley
Plays "Rick Winston" in "Madison"
Other Credits:
Suckers (1999)
• Howling V - The Rebirth (1989)

Vincent Ventresca
Plays "Walker Grief" in "Madison"
Other Credits:
The Learning Curve (2001)
• Looking For Lola (1997)
• Romy and Michele's High School Reunion (1997)
• The Learning Curve (2001)

John M. Watson, Sr.
Plays "Walter" in "Madison"
Other Credits:
Soul Food (1997)
• Opportunity Knocks (1990)

John Mellencamp
Actor
Concert For America/Farm Aid (2002)
• Falling From Grace (1992)
• Vision Shared - A Tribute to Woody Guthrie and Leadbelly (1990)

Madison -- Hydroplane Heritage - *Fred Farley & Ron Harsin*

Voice
- Madison

Singer/Songwriter
- Many hit songs

Kristina Anapau
Plays "Tami" in "Madison"

James Andelin
Plays "Merle" in "Madison"

Reed Diamond
Plays "Skip" in "Madison"

The Making Of The Movie

Production of this movie took place in the late summer and early fall of 1999 in Los Angeles, San Diego, Chicago, Miami, California (Lake Castaic and Long Beach) and in Columbus and Madison, Indiana.

Jake Lloyd on film location in Madison, Indiana

Madison -- Hydroplane Heritage - Fred Farley & Ron Harsin

Todd Yarling, his nephew Samuel and his brother Ky on the movie's MISS BUDWEISER.

One of the camera crew, this guy ended the film day in Madison with a major sunburn.

While the turbine engine hydroplanes were holding their race, the film crews had to sit and wait. Between heats of competition, the vintage 1971 style hydroplanes took to the river and race for the cameras.

Another camera from the banks of the Ohio

There were cameras placed on both the Indiana and the Kentucky sides of the Ohio River. The filming involved radio contact between the director, film crews and drivers of the vintage hydroplanes.

Madison -- Hydroplane Heritage - Fred Farley & Ron Harsin

This helicopter film crew flew just a few feet above the boats to shoot some of the scenes.

The helicopter film crew flew from the Madison Municipal Airport to the race course and film the boats and crowds of people on the river banks watching as spectators.

The helicopter film crew flew <u>under</u> the Madison/Milton bridge for some of the shots.

Madison -- Hydroplane Heritage - Fred Farley & Ron Harsin

Just a few feet above the MISS MADISON

Many times during the filming, the helicopter was so close to the boat that a person standing on the boat could have reached up and touched the bottom of the helicopter.

The hydroplanes were modified for the movie so an actual hydroplane driver could sit in the front cockpit and drive the boat, while the actor sat in the back seat for the filming. In this picture, Todd Yarling prepares to take the MISS MADISON driver (checking out the competition ?) and the MISS BUDWEISER out for a run.

Madison -- Hydroplane Heritage - Fred Farley & Ron Harsin

Todd Yarling (front) drives the twin cockpit MISS BUDWEISER (and the actor William Shockley) (back) out onto the race course for a movie scene.

Actor Jim Caviezel in the cockpit. Note the camera mount. Although not visible in this shot, the back of the boat is painted as the MISS MADISON, and the front is painted as the MISS BUDWEISER.

Madison -- Hydroplane Heritage - Fred Farley & Ron Harsin

The real MISS BUDWEISER gives chase to the 1/2 MISS BUDWEISER, 1/2 MISS MADISON

The "real" MISS MADISON had a few limited scenes in the movie. The "real" 1971 Gold Cup winner was in the process of being refurbished during the filming and could not be used for the movie. Shown here without a sponson.

Madison -- Hydroplane Heritage - Fred Farley & Ron Harsin

Building a sponson for the movie.

The "CAT'S PRIDE".

There has never been a hydroplane on the circuit with this name, however, it is rumored that a "kitty litter" company helped sponsor the making of the movie. Posing in front of the "CAT'S PRIDE" are: (back) John Freeman, Roger Newton and Peter Orten from the Hydroplane & Raceboat Museum. (front) Dr. Ken Muscatel and David Williams, both with driving duties.

Madison -- Hydroplane Heritage - Fred Farley & Ron Harsin

The actual 1971 MISS BUDWEISER was a "spoon front" brown painted boat. This MISS BUDWEISER was planned for the movie, however, Roger & Gerry Kingen's Bud had carburetor problems and was replaced with the red "pickle fork" Budweiser in the movie. If you look closely while watching the movie, there are a few scenes with this brown boat.

Setting up a scene for the movie. In this picture, the director Bill Bindley can be seen on the right giving instructions.

Madison -- Hydroplane Heritage - Fred Farley & Ron Harsin

The SAVAIRS MIST was painted as the MISS MADISON and used in the movie. The actual 1971 Gold Cup winning MISS MADISON was in the process of being restored and was not available for the movie.

Trivia buffs: The real MISS MADISON appears in a few scenes of the movie, look for it in the movie without a sponson (and without fire burns) while being pulled down main street.

SAVAIRS MIST

Madison -- Hydroplane Heritage - Fred Farley & Ron Harsin

The movie version of the MISS MADISON in the pit area.

The movie version of the MISS MADISON preparing for a scene. Note the two swimmers near the boat. The swimmers would attempt to keep the boat in the exact position for a camera shot.

Madison -- Hydroplane Heritage - Fred Farley & Ron Harsin

The movie version of the MISS MADISON continues to prepare for the scene.

The PAY 'n PAK'S LIL BUZZARD painted as the ATLAS VAN LINES II and used in the movie. The actual ATLAS boat that ran during the 1971 Gold Cup race was a pickle fork front design. A picture of the real ATLAS can be found later in this book.

Madison -- Hydroplane Heritage - Fred Farley & Ron Harsin

PAY 'n PAK'S LIL BUZZARD.

THE SMOOTHER MOVER painted as the MISS BUDWEISER for early scenes in the movie.

This is the style of the BUDWEISER boat that actually ran during the 1971 Gold Cup race. A picture of the real MISS BUDWEISER can be found later in this book.

Madison -- Hydroplane Heritage - Fred Farley & Ron Harsin

The SMOOTHER MOVER

This boat was a former MISS BUDWEISER in 1980, however, it was not the MISS BUDWEISER that ran during the 1971 Gold Cup Race. This "RED" MISS BUDWEISER appeared in the majority of the movie scenes.

Madison -- Hydroplane Heritage - Fred Farley & Ron Harsin

The MISS MADISON and the ATLAS VAN LINES do battle for the movie. Listening in on the movie company radio frequency, a person would hear instructions to the boat drivers, telling them to pull in front of one of the other boats, or to drop back behind the other boats.

Another scene where the MISS MADISON and the ATLAS VAN LINES compete for the movie. All of the instructions were broadcast so the cameras could capture the desired boat's position as it raced against the other boats in the movie.

The ATLAS VAN LINES and the MISS BUDWEISER preparing to go under the Madison/Milton bridge.

TEMPEST

TEMPEST was painted as the TOWNE CLUB and repainted as the CAT'S PRIDE for use in the movie ".

Madison -- Hydroplane Heritage - Fred Farley & Ron Harsin

Todd Yarling and his two children in the movie's MISS BUDWEISER.

Todd Yarling - Actual driver of the MISS BUDWEISER in the movie. The 1962 NOTRE DAME was sold and became THE SMOOTHER MOVER. This same boat was repainted for use as the 1971 NOTRE DAME in the movie.

Boats Used In The Movie

SAVAIR'S MIST painted as the MISS MADISON

PAY 'n PAK'S LIL BUZZARD painted as the ATLAS VAN LINES (Note: the 1971 boat was a pickle fork nose boat)

THE SMOOTHER MOVER painted as MISS BUDWEISER (brown boat)

MISS BUDWEISER used in the movie as the "RED" MISS BUDWEISER (Note: the 1971 boat was a spoon nose brown boat)

Movie Props

A movie prop, this racing program shows the same cover as the original 1971 program.

This newspaper was created specifically for the movie.

A "Madison" movie crew shirt. Embroidery for this shirt and the crew uniforms was provided by "Embroidery Unlimited" in Madison, Indiana.

Madison -- Hydroplane Heritage - Fred Farley & Ron Harsin

McCormick Lane - Madison, Indiana

Madison -- Hydroplane Heritage - Fred Farley & Ron Harsin

Madison -- Hydroplane Heritage - Fred Farley & Ron Harsin

Chapter Eight
1971 Madison Gold Cup Race
The Original Story

MISS MADISON's victory in the 1971 APBA Gold Cup on home waters in Madison, Indiana, ranks as one of racing's most memorable milestones. After years of countless retelling, the MISS MADISON Gold Cup story has indeed reached mythic proportions.

The popular press account tells of MISS MADISON, an aging underdog of a boat, suddenly and miraculously coming alive on July 4, 1971, trouncing its well-financed opposition in the race of races. Here was a modern day David and Goliath -- the hydro upset of the century -- in the most memorable aquatic shootout since the Monitor and the Merrimac.

All of this hyperbole, of course, is pure poppycock. MISS MADISON was not the thousand-to-one long shot of popular legend. On the contrary, she was a bona-fide contender.

At the time of the 1971 Gold Cup, it was easy for media representatives to get caught up in the emotion of the moment. I know that I certainly did. The race was the answer to a sports reporter's dream. The inevitable reaction: "What a scoop. I can't overwrite this one."

Unfortunately, quite a few columnists got carried away in the euphoria of the MISS MADISON triumph. I was as guilty as anyone. The article I wrote for Raceboat Industry News on the 1971 Gold Cup was as badly written as anything I've done in 36 years of covering Unlimiteds. I'm not proud of it.

Okay. I was a rabid fan of MISS MADISON. The driver, Jim McCormick, was a personal friend and this was my first of many visits to the picturesque Ohio River town that would soon become my home away from home. Small wonder then that my initial report on the race was something less than objective.

In the years that followed, I toyed with the idea of writing a truly definitive account of the race for posterity. The opportunity to do so presented itself in late 1983. That was when my friend David Taylor, editor of the Madison Regatta souvenir program book, asked for my help on the 1984 edition.

I worked all winter on the MISS MADISON Gold Cup article. It totaled approximately 5000 words on nineteen typewritten pages, one of my longer efforts. Most of my stories average around 1500 or 2000 words, but this one was very special.

My thanks go to David Greene and Philip Haldeman, both of the APBA Unlimited Historical Committee. I received a lot of valuable input from Dave and Phil that I greatly appreciate.

For what it's worth, I consider "MISS MADISON, The Gold Cup Champion" to be the single best article I've ever written for publication, out of the hundreds that I've done since 1962. I really gave it my all. I wanted to set the record straight about the second MISS MADISON being a competitive boat from late-1970 onward. But mainly, I did it for the driver and crew. I just wrote it down. They're the ones who went out there and did it. I wanted them to be able to re-experience their magnificent achievement.

I believe I achieved my goal as all the surviving team members told me they enjoyed reading my story.

I also wrote it for the fans. For those who were fortunate enough to be there, hopefully they can return, in the mind's eye, to that thrilling day in 1971. For those who were not yet born in 1971, perhaps they too will be able to feel some of the same emotions as if they had been there, cheering the Miss Madison on to gold and glory.

MISS MADISON
The Gold Cup Champion

No one who attended the fabulous 1971 APBA Gold Cup Regatta in Madison, Indiana, will ever forget it. That was when MISS MADISON, the world's only community-owned and sponsored Unlimited hydroplane, confounded the oddsmakers, winning the race of races before the hometown crowd.

The MISS MADISON's richly sentimental triumph on that memorable July 4 was a historic one on several levels. Not since the 1965 Dixie Cup at Guntersville, Alabama, had the sun-bleached MISS MADISON scored a victory. It was pilot Jim McCormick's first win ever in the Unlimited Class. The MISS MADISON was built in 1959 and first entered competition in 1960, thereby making her the only Unlimited hydroplane ever to win a Gold Cup eleven years after its competitive debut. Not since mandatory qualifications began in 1949, had a Gold Cup winner placed lower than fourth on the qualifying speed ladder. MISS MADISON was seventh.

The 1971 event also marked the first and only time a community-owned boat has won the Gold Cup. Not since

1966 had the American Power Boat Association's Crown Jewel been won by a boat with Allison, rather than Rolls-Royce aircraft power. The MISS MADISON of 1971 also represented the end of an era. She was the last Unlimited hydroplane with the old-style rear cockpit, forward engine, shovel-nosed bow configuration to achieve victory.

The hull that became the Gold Cup-winning MISS MADISON was designed and built by Les Staudacher of Kawkawlin, Michigan. Staudacher had previously constructed such successful contenders as MISS PEPSI, GALE V, TEMPO VIII, MISS THRIFTWAY and HAWAII KAI III. The future MISS MADISON measured 30 feet in length with a 12-foot beam. Made of marine plywood and aluminum, she tipped the scales at close to 7000 lb. in racing trim.

Les Staudacher

The craft made its competitive debut at the 1960 Detroit Memorial Regatta on the Detroit River. She was called NITROGEN TOO at that time and owned by Industrialist, Samuel F. DuPont, of Wilmington, Delaware. The TOO was a teammate of DuPont's original NITROGEN, another Allison-powered Staudacher creation, constructed in 1957.

Driven primarily by Ron Musson of Akron, Ohio, the NITROGEN TOO performed no better than average in the early part of the 1960 campaign, running well behind the speedsters of the era. Still, she performed well enough for a nomination to the United States Harmsworth Challenge Team along with her sister ship and with Joe Schoenith's GALE V.

In the Harmsworth International Race on the Bay of Quinte at Picton, Ontario, NITROGEN TOO led the first lap of the Second Heat, posting a speed of 123 miles per hour on the 5-mile oval course. This was only 3 mph under the world record set by the Canadian defender, and eventual Harmsworth winner, MISS SUPERTEST III.

At the 1960 Silver Cup in Detroit, NITROGEN TOO won a surprising and impressive victory, beating the favored MISS THRIFTWAY and averaging 101.919 miles an hour for the 45-mile distance. Leadfoot Ron Musson would not be denied, leading MISS THRIFTWAY pilot, Bill Muncey all the way in the Final Championship Heat. The DuPont team's triumph was all the more remarkable, considering that MISS THRIFTWAY used the more-powerful Rolls-Royce Merlin engine. NITROGEN TOO, on the other hand, ran a basically stock Allison power source.

At season's end, NITROGEN and NITROGEN TOO had tied down second and third positions in the 1960 National Points chase, behind MISS THRIFTWAY in a field of 29 boats. In addition to her Silver Cup achievement, the TOO had taken second place in the Madison Regatta and third in the Buffalo Launch Club event.

In 1961, Sam DuPont withdrew from competition and donated the older NITROGEN to the city of Madison, Indiana. The name was changed to MISS MADISON, Graham Heath of Madison became the crew chief of an all-volunteer crew and Marion Cooper of Louisville, Kentucky, signed on as the

Madison -- Hydroplane Heritage - Fred Farley & Ron Harsin

driver.

The original MISS MADISON took a fifth in its first race, the 1961 Detroit Memorial. Later in the season, the team scored a hard fought victory in the second division Seattle Trophy Race at the Seafair World's Championship Regatta on Lake Washington. The following year, Cooper, Heath and company took fourth in the Spirit of Detroit Trophy and third in the Indiana Governor's Cup.

In 1963, the first MISS MADISON ended its career where it had begun -- in Detroit. During trials for the Gold Cup Race, MISS MADISON was completely destroyed and pilot Morlan Visel was seriously injured.

Not to worry, the city of Madison was not about to lose its floating chamber of commerce. The Ohio River townspeople already had another hull, the NITROGEN TOO, waiting in the wings, which had likewise been acquired from Mr. DuPont.

The "new" MISS MADISON, which was to become a racing legend, made its initial appearance in competition at the 1963 Madison Regatta. She placed fifth in the Indiana Govemor's Cup, driven by George "Buddy" Byers of Columbus, Ohio, a champion 7-Litre Class pilot.

The craft had a big year in '64. She gave an extremely consistent performance that allowed her to finish second in the National Point Standings. Although she didn't win a race, MISS MADISON ran better than in her initial season as NITROGEN TOO. She was runner-up in the Dixie Cup at Guntersville, Alabama and the Dakota Cup at New Town, North Dakota. MISS MADISON also took third place in the Diamond Cup at Coeur d'Alene, Idaho, the Seafair Trophy at Seattle and the President's Cup at Washington, D.C.

Everywhere she competed, MISS MADISON served as the best ambassador of good will the tiny Mid-Western town ever had. Indeed, the city of Madison became a household word from coast to coast, thanks to the fast-moving

U-6, her intrepid driver Buddy Byers and her masterful crew chief, Graham Heath.

In 1965, the MISS MADISON racing team posted its first major victory with a 102.746 mile an hour come-from-behind triumph at the Dixie Cup. MISS MADISON entered the Final Heat on Guntersville Lake with two second place finishes in the preliminary action. Sprinting toward the starting line, Byers realized that he and the other drivers were too early and in danger of "jumping the gun." Buddy eased off on the throttle and wisely resisted the impulse to follow when the rest of the field thundered past him. Sure enough, front runners MISS U.S. 5, NOTRE DAME and TAHOE MISS all crossed prematurely and incurred a one-lap penalty. Byers backpedaled to a legal start, cruised to an easy victory and wound up with 1000 accumulated points, 73 more than the second place finisher MARINER TOO, driven by Warner Gardner.

For the balance of the 1965 campaign, MISS MADISON generally failed to show the consistency or the speed of the previous year. Exceptions to this summary included the U-6's 106 mile an hour heat at the Seattle Gold Cup and her second place overall finish in the San Diego Cup.

Jim McCormick of Owensboro, Kentucky, made his Unlimited Class debut as driver of the community-owned entry in 1966, replacing Buddy Byers who had signed on to drive Bill Harrah's TAHOE MISS. By this time, Graham Heath had also left the team to accept the position of crew chief for Jim Ranger's new, Detroit-based, MY GYPSY organization.

The reorganized MISS MADISON team had a mediocre year at best in 1966 and had difficulty qualifying for final heats. Their highest finishes were a third at the Tampa Suncoast Cup and a fourth at the Madison Regatta.

Madison -- Hydroplane Heritage - Fred Farley & Ron Harsin

MY GYPSY

Following a reduced schedule of races in 1967-68 with Ed O'Halloran of Detroit, Michigan, as driver, the craft improved on its 1966 performance but was simply not the contender she had been under the helmsmanship of Buddy Byers. The highest finish during the O'Halloran years was a second place in the 1967 Suncoast Cup on Tampa Bay.

In 1969, the now-experienced, Jim McCormick returned to the cockpit. But even with the change in drivers, the boat's performance did not improve. A third at the hometown Madison Regatta was the team's highest finish. Indeed, the glory days of 1964-65 seemed light years away.

MISS MADISON almost missed the 1970 campaign entirely having been involved in a highway accident in Georgia while enroute to the first race of the season in Tampa, Florida. Pulled off the circuit, the stricken craft underwent repairs by original builder Les Staudacher. In retrospect, the mishap was probably a blessing. Staudacher used the occasion to go through the entire hull and fix several things in addition to the highway accident damage that might otherwise have gone unnoticed.

The end result was an improved contender when MISS MADISON returned to action a month later. Had the National Championship been determined that year solely on the results of the five races the MISS MADISON did enter, discounting the three that she missed, the team would have finished fourth instead of sixth.

MISS MADISON defeated the highly regarded Tommy "Tucker" Fults and PAY 'n PAK'S LIL BUZZARD in Heat 1-B at Madison, which was a surprise. The U-6 also showed a lot of class, with a definite increase in speed, when she and McCormick trounced the favored Bill Muncey and MYR SHEET METAL in both Heats 1-C and 3-A of the season-concluding San Diego Gold Cup.

At year's end, MISS MADISON was running the best of her long career and giving the better-than-average performance that was expected of her. She could make the front runners work for it and could run with them on occasion.

But the general consensus at the outset of 1971 was that only a newer hull and more power would put the U-6 team in the winner's circle. Nevertheless, the MISS MADISON organization decided to stay with their eleven, going on twelve year old craft for one more season.

The 1971 campaign started with a new race, the Champion Spark Plug Regatta, on Biscayne Bay at Miami Marine Stadium. MISS MADISON was leading in both of her preliminary heats but was forced to drop back due to a fuel mixture problem in section 1-A and a faulty supercharger in 2-B. Not to be denied a spot in the finale, the volunteer crew members proved their mettle by performing a complete engine change in less than thirty minutes. Pilot McCormick then proceeded to take second spot in both the Third Heat and the overall standings behind Dean Chenoweth and the MISS BUDWEISER.

MISS MADISON continued in the Champion Regatta, a resurgence that had begun in the last race of 1970. No longer was the U-6 thought of as a slightly better-than-average boat that was merely along for the ride. The MISS MADISON was now regarded as a viable contender. However, the team was still short on money and horsepower and most people still refused to take the community-owned boat seriously.

Moving on to the President's Cup contest on the Potomac River, MISS MADISON won her first two heats convincingly. She defeated the likes of Billy Schumacher in PRIDE OF PAY 'n PAK, Leif Borgersen in HALLMARK HOMES and Billy Sterett, Jr., in NOTRE DAME, each of which had a millionaire owner and used the more powerful Rolls-Royce Merlin engine.

Prior to the finale, MISS MADISON and Jim McCormick were not an illogical choice to win the race, based upon their strong showing in the preliminary action. Charging into the first turn of the Championship Heat, however, the U-6 was hosed down by the roostertails of HALLMARK HOMES and the eventual winner, ATLAS VAN LINES I, handled by Bill Muncey. McCormick managed to restart and take a disappointing fourth behind HALLMARK, ATLAS I and MISS BUDWEISER, although he managed to overtake and outrun PRIDE OF PAY 'n PAK by a wide margin.

The MISS MADISON team won the overall second place President's Cup trophy for 1971 and had the satisfaction of running both the fastest 15-mile heat and the swiftest 45-mile race of the contest. But driver McCormick was bitterly discouraged. He had missed victory by a scant 31 points and was beginning to wonder if winning a race was, perhaps, an impossible dream.

In the Kentucky Governor's Cup at Owensboro, MISS MADISON did not improve on her two previous performances, taking an overall third behind ATLAS VAN LINES I and PRIDE OF PAY 'n PAK. The U-6 challenged MISS BUDWEISER for the lead in Heat 2, but otherwise her performance was undistinguished.

At the Horace E. Dodge Cup in Detroit, MISS MADISON ran head-to-head with Terry Sterett and ATLAS VAN LINES II (the former MYR SHEET METAL) in the

Madison -- Hydroplane Heritage - Fred Farley & Ron Harsin

First Heat, despite rough water. On the last lap, Sterett moved ahead of McCormick and maintained this advantage to win by three boat lengths.

In the Second Heat, MISS MADISON broke down and recorded her first DNF (Did Not Finish) of the year. Consequently, the U-6 was ineligible for the finale. Still, MISS MADISON was running the best of her almost ended career.

The Thunderboat trail now led to Madison, Indiana, which was steeped in a competitive tradition that dated back to 1911. As things developed, the city's 60th boat racing anniversary story would have amazed a fiction writer. No publisher would have accepted a make-believe script on the race.

For the first time since 1951, the Indiana Governor's Cup shared the spotlight with the APBA Gold Cup, power boating's Crown Jewel, which had never been run in a town as small as Madison. Due to a technicality and a misunderstanding, the $30,000 bid for the race by the sponsoring Madison Regatta, Inc., was the only one submitted to the Gold Cup Contest Board in time.

For ten years, the volunteer MISS MADISON mechanical crew had tried to win the hometown race without success. They faced an uphill fight in 1971 and they knew it. In the first four races of the season, MISS BUDWEISER and ATLAS VAN LINES I had both scored two solid victories apiece.

ATLAS VAN LINES II, a five-race winner in 1969-70, was likewise a formidable contender. Having been her team's number one entry during the three previous years, the ATLAS VAN LINES II's performance had suffered little in her secondary role with Terry Sterett in the cockpit.

Also not to be overlooked in the pre-race figuring at the Madison Gold Cup were the HALLMARK HOMES, the NOTRE DAME and the PRIDE OF PAY 'n PAK.

Madison -- Hydroplane Heritage - Fred Farley & Ron Harsin

Madison to host the Gold Cup. 1971 Madison Regatta Queen - Carol Eggeman

    HALLMARK was having a difficult season but nevertheless had championship credentials, being the former 1967-68 Gold Cup and National High Point-winning MISS BARDAHL.
    NOTRE DAME, a virtual copy of the HALLMARK HOMES, had a reputation of being a fast competitive boat, although she had never won a race.
    PAY 'n PAK was likewise having an uneven 1971 campaign. The PAK sported a radical new design. She was wider, flatter, less box-shaped, had a pickle-forked bow configuration and had performed admirably on occasion. The craft had experienced a disastrous 1970 season, but there were

Madison -- Hydroplane Heritage - Fred Farley & Ron Harsin

a few who staunchly believed that if PRIDE OF PAY 'n PAK ever had the "bugs" ironed out of her, she would revolutionize the sport and render obsolete all top contenders of the previous twenty years.

Several days before the race, Jim McCormick placed a crucial telephone call to Reno, Nevada. He requested, and obtained, the services of two of the finest Allison engine specialists in the sport. Harry Volpi and Everett Adams of the defunct HARRAH'S CLUB racing team flew to Madison and worked in the pits alongside U-6 regulars Tony Steinhardt, Bob Humphrey, Dave Stewart, Keith Hand and Russ Willey. Volpi and Adams are credited with perfecting the MISS MADISON's water-alcohol injection system.

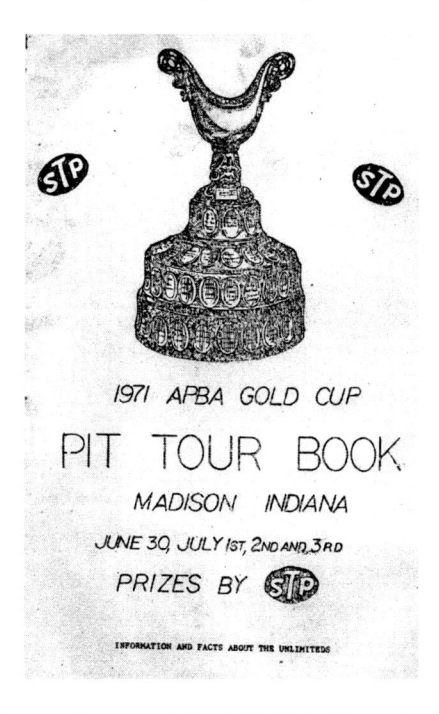

Front Cover of the 1971 Pit Tour Book

Madison -- Hydroplane Heritage - Fred Farley & Ron Harsin

The 1971 Gold Cup Race

Race day, July 4, 1971, dawned bright and warm with ten qualified boats prepared to do competitive battle. A crowd of 110,000 fans literally choked the small Mid-Western town of 13,000. The river conditions were good, but MISS MADISON was down to her last engine, having blown the other in trials. This put the U-6 people at a distinct disadvantage, because, at that time, the Gold Cup Race consisted of four 15-mile heats instead of the usual three.

The race was less than thirty seconds old when HALLMARK HOMES disintegrated in a geyser of spray and sank in the first turn of Heat 1-A, after encountering the roostertail of ATLAS VAN LINES I. HALLMARK pilot Leif Borgersen escaped injury, but his boat was totaled.

The random heat draw by Guy Lombardo and WAVE TV Sports Director, Ed Kallay

MISS MADISON was drawn into Heat 1-B along with TOWNE CLUB, MISS TIMEX, THE SMOOTHER MOVER and ATLAS VAN LINES II. During the warm-up period, THE SMOOTHER MOVER joined HALLMARK HOMES at the bottom of the river when her supercharger blew and punched a hole in the MOVER'S underside.

MISS MADISON had the lead at the end of lap one but was then passed by ATLAS II. On lap three, the Fred Alter-chauffeured TOWNE CLUB began to challenge MISS MADISON for second place. McCormick and Alter see-sawed back and forth for several laps and brought the crowd to its feet. MISS MADISON managed to outrun the TOWNE CLUB and hung on for second place points behind the front-running ATLAS II.

The MISS MADISON and the TOWNE CLUB do battle in Heat 1-B of the 1971 Gold Cup Race.

For the second round of preliminaries, MISS MADISON matched skills with MISS BUDWEISER, NOTRE DAME and ATLAS I in Heat 2-B. Bill Muncey reached the first turn first with ATLAS I, followed by MISS MADISON. BUDWEISER and NOTRE DAME were both watered down by Muncey's roostertail, causing both to go dead in the water. ATLAS I widened its lead over the field down the first backstretch and in the ensuing laps, while MISS MADISON settled into a safe second. MISS BUDWEISER immediately restarted and followed MISS MADISON around the course in third place. NOTRE DAME also managed to restart but only after being lapped by the field.

At the end of 15 miles, Muncey and ATLAS I received the green flag instead of the checkered flag, indicating a one lap penalty for a foul against MISS BUDWEISER and NOTRE DAME in the first turn for violation of the overlap rule. This moved MISS MADISON from second to first position in the corrected order of finish. MISS BUDWEISER was given second place and ATLAS I wound up officially in third after running seven laps before NOTRE DAME could finish six.

Bill Muncey learns of the imposed penalty.

After another random draw, MISS MADISON found herself in Heat 3-B along with ATLAS II, NOTRE DAME and PRIDE OF PAY 'n PAK.

As Bill Muncey was preparing to drive ATLAS I before Heat 3-A, he received word that Referee Bill Newton had put him on probation for the next three races of the season. The probation had resulted not only from the foul against the field in Heat 2-B but also from the cumulative effect of similar infractions by Muncey in 1970 at Seattle and

San Diego. The consequence of the probation was that any further violations by Muncey would result in an indefinite suspension from racing.

Unperturbed, Muncey made a good start in Heat 3-A and was chasing Dean Chenoweth and MISS BUDWEISER down the first backstretch when ATLAS I sheared off her right sponson and started taking on water. Bill frantically tried to steer his wounded craft toward the bank on the Kentucky side of the river but was unable to do so. ATLAS VAN LINES I rolled over on its side about 100 feet from shore and slipped beneath the surface, forcing Muncey to abandon ship. Now, three boats rested at the bottom of the Ohio.

ATLAS VAN LINES I loses the right sponson in Heat 3-A

Bill Muncey being pulled from the water after the ATLAS VAN LINES I sinks to the bottom of the Ohio River.

Terry Sterett and ATLAS II entered the first turn of Heat 3-B in the lead and stayed there, but MISS MADISON kept nipping at their heels. PRIDE OF PAY 'n PAK, running in third, tried to overtake MISS MADISON but the U-6 pulled away to maintain second position. On the last lap, MISS MADISON came on hard to finish only two seconds behind ATLAS II and four seconds ahead of PAY 'n PAK.

Miss Madison vs. Atlas Van Lines II

After three grueling sets of elimination heats, the five qualifiers for the final go-around were, Atlas II with 1100 accumulated points, MISS MADISON with 1000 points, PRIDE OF PAY 'n PAK with 869, TOWNE CLUB with 750 and MISS BUDWEISER with 700.

As the sun started to set on that historic July 4, the race for the Gold Cup and the Governor's Cup boiled down to ATLAS VAN LINES II and Miss Madison. MISS MADISON had to make up a deficit of 100 points in order to win the championship. To do this, the U-6 would have to finish first in the final 15-mile, moment of truth. This appeared rather unlikely since the combination of Terry Sterett and ATLAS II had bested the team of Jim McCormick and MISS MADISON in each of their four previous match-ups that season, twice on the Ohio River and twice the previous weekend on the Detroit River.

As the field took to the water for the last time, some of the hometown fans hung on to the hope that perhaps ATLAS

Madison -- Hydroplane Heritage - Fred Farley & Ron Harsin

II would fail to start and, thereby, allow the local favorite to win the big race by default. But that was not to be. As McCormick wheeled MISS MADISON out onto the 2-1/2 mile course, there was Sterett, starting up and pulling out of the pit area right behind him. Thus, as the final minutes and seconds ticked away, the die was cast. If McCormick hoped to achieve his first career victory on this day, he would have to earn it the hard way.

Meanwhile, the ABC "Wide World Of Sports" television crew members, who were there taping the race for a delayed national broadcast, decided among themselves that Terry Sterett was a shoo-in for the title. Accordingly, they set up their camera equipment in the ATLAS II's pit area in anticipation of interviewing the victorious Sterett when he returned to the dock.

All five finalists were on the course and running. Moments before the one-minute gun, MISS MADISON was observed cruising down the front straightaway in front of the pit area. Then, abruptly, McCormick altered course, making a hard left turn into the infield. He sped across course, making a bee-line for the entrance buoy of the upper corner. His strategy was obvious. McCormick wanted the inside lane to force the other boats to run a wider and longer course.

As the field charged underneath the Madison/Milton Bridge, four of the five boats were closely bunched with Fred Alter's TOWNE CLUB on the extreme outside, skirting the shoreline. MISS MADISON had lane one; ATLAS VAN LINES II had lane two and was slightly in the lead when the starting gun fired.

Sprinting toward the first turn, PRIDE OF PAY 'n PAK spun out. ATLAS II made it into and out of the turn in front with MISS MADISON close behind on the inside. As the field entered the first backstretch, the order was ATLAS, MADISON, BUDWEISER, PAY 'n PAK and TOWNE CLUB.

Madison -- Hydroplane Heritage - Fred Farley & Ron Harsin

The start of a 1971 Gold Cup heat

Then McCormick made his move. After having run a steady conservative race all day long, "Gentleman Jim" slammed the accelerator to the floor. The boat took off like a shot and thundered past Terry Sterett as if his rival were tied to the dock.

The actual moment that MISS MADISON passed ATLAS VAN LINES II in the Final Heat.

The partisan crowd screamed in unison, "GO. GO. GO."

Even hardened veterans of racing were dumbfounded. An aging, under-powered, under-financed museum piece was

Madison -- Hydroplane Heritage - Fred Farley & Ron Harsin

leading the race and leaving the rest of the field to wallow in its wake.

McCormick whipped MISS MADISON around the upper turn expertly and sped under the bridge and back down the river to the start/finish line. It was one down and five laps to go. The ATLAS, the BUDWEISER and the PAY 'n PAK were closely bunched at this point as they followed MISS MADISON around the buoys.

The crowd was going absolutely wild. In lap two, McCormick increased his lead. In lap three, he extended his advantage even more. It dawned on the "Wide World Of Sports" crew that an upset was in the making. Frantically, the ABC-TV technicians scrambled out of the ATLAS pit area and hustled their camera gear over to the MISS MADISON pits.

Out on the race course, Sterett had shaken free of BUDWEISER and PAY 'n PAK and was going all out after MISS MADISON. He was fast on the straightaways, but not as fast as McCormick. The ATLAS cornered well, but not as well as the U-6.

MISS MADISON was running flawlessly, her 26-year old Allison engine not missing a beat. Jim McCormick was driving the race of his life. Together, the boat and driver made an inspired combination. Bonnie McCormick, Jim's wife, who had averted her eyes during the first few laps, was now concentrating fully on the action, cheering her husband on at the top of her lungs.

MISS MADISON received the green flag, indicating one more lap to the checkered flag and victory. By now, the community-owned craft had a decisive lead. Sterett was beaten and he knew it. The ATLAS pilot could only hope against hope that a mechanical problem or a driving error would slow the MISS MADISON down.

But that didn't happen. McCormick made one last perfect turn. The MISS MADISON'S roostertail kicked skyward. The boat streaked under the bridge, past Bennett's dock and over the finish line, adding a new chapter to American sports legend, as pandemonium broke loose on the shore.

Firebells rang, automobile horns sounded and the spectators went out of their minds with delight. Everybody, it seemed, was a U-6 fan and whether they lived there or not, a Madisonian. Even members of rival teams were applauding the outcome of this modern day Horatio Alger story.

Jim McCormick waved at the crowd on the victory lap of the 1971 Gold Cup race.

MISS MADISON had beaten ATLAS VAN LINES II by 16.3 seconds in the Final Heat and was 4.2 seconds swifter for the overall 60 miles. McCormick and Sterett had tied with 1400 points a piece in the four heats of racing. According to Unlimited Class rules, a point tie is broken by the order of finish in the last heat of the day. The U-6 Team won it all. This included an engraved plate, that would read MISS MADISON, to be added to the rows of gleaming testimonials to the conquests of Gar Wood, George Reis, Danny Foster,

Stan Sayres, Bill Muncey and others.

It was the biggest day in the history of Madison, Indiana. It was Unlimited Hydroplane racing at its best. It was a victory for the amateur, for the common man, a triumph that everyone could claim as his own. Not since the SLO-MO-SHUN days in Seattle during the 1950s had such an outpouring of civic emotion occurred at a Gold Cup Race with people celebrating in the streets.

Jim McCormick pulls MISS MADISON up to the pits after winning the 1971 Gold Cup race.

Jim McCormick and crew members Tony Steinhardt and Dave Stewart celebrate on the boat deck.

Deliriously happy, MISS MADISON crew members carried pilot McCormick on their shoulders to the Judges' Stand. Veteran boat racer George N. Davis, a mentor of

Madison -- Hydroplane Heritage - Fred Farley & Ron Harsin

McCormick's during Jim's 280 Class career, wept unashamedly at this, his protege's moment of triumph.

After receiving the Gold Cup from 1946 winner, Guy Lombardo and the Governor's Cup from Indiana Governor Edgar Whitcomb, a tired but happy McCormick explained his race strategy to the assembled legion of awe-struck media representatives.

"We planned to take it easy in the early heats and then let it all hang out in the finals."

Jim McCormick, Mike McCormick, Tony Steinhardt, Indiana Governor Edgar Whitcomb and Guy Lombardo.

Holding up the Gold Cup for all to see

Madison -- Hydroplane Heritage - Fred Farley & Ron Harsin

Regatta Queen Carol Eggeman, Guy Lombardo, Jim McCormick and Indiana Governor Edgar Whitcomb.

Jim McCormick gets a hug from Madison Mayor Donald Vaughn

Jim McCormick with his parents.

McCormick was the first to give credit where credit was due. He quickly acknowledged that without the mechanical prowess of his volunteer pit crew, victory would have been impossible. "These guys have been working their hearts out getting ready for this. They deserve all the credit."

The MISS MADISON crew received the Markt A. Lytle Sportsmanship Trophy at the Gold Cup Awards Banquet, where tribute was also paid to the two former HARRAH'S CLUB team members, Volpi and Adams, for their invaluable help in winning "the big one".

"Gentleman Jim" McCormick, who had achieved his "Impossible Dream," was the hero of the day and he gratefully acknowledged the enthusiasm of the crowd. For several hours after the trophy presentation, McCormick, still in his driving suit, remained at the Judges' Stand, signing his name for one and all. "Let the people come," he said. "I'll sign autographs as long as I can write." It was the perfect ending to a perfect day.

As the spectators and participants drifted back to their own lives, one thought was uppermost in the minds of many: "Was it all a dream, or did today really happen?"

Madison -- Hydroplane Heritage - Fred Farley & Ron Harsin

Dreams Come True As Miss Madison Picks Up Gold Cup

McCormick Pulls Off Big Upset

Madison Courier news item.

The 1971 Madison Gold Cup Champions

The 1971 Gold Cup

The Very Next Race

Yes, it did happen. It happened again three weeks later on the Columbia River at the Tri-Cities, Washington. MISS MADISON driver McCormick and crew members Steinhardt, Stewart, Humphrey, Hand and Willey made the incredible seem commonplace. They won the sixth annual Atomic Cup Race and, in so doing, moved from second to first place in the National Season Points chase.

Entering the Final Heat in fourth place in regatta points with two second-place finishes, MISS MADISON was again lightly regarded as a title threat. The boat's nitrous oxide system, which gives the craft an added burst of speed coming off the corners, had failed to function during the first two heats. In fact, the crew wasn't even certain if the engine was going to start for the finale. But, in McCormick's words, "We got it all together," and not a moment too soon.

Most attention centered on Billy Schumacher in the PRIDE OF PAY 'n PAK and Bill Muncey in the now repaired ATLAS VAN LINES I, who led the field with only 100 points separating them. The futuristic PAY 'n PAK looked especially formidable that day and seemed on the verge of coming into her own. However, many experts were still siding with ATLAS I to win due to that boat's superior record on the Eastern tour.

Again, MISS MADISON moved to the inside lane before the start and stayed there. The first corner was tight with four of the five finalists closely bunched. MISS MADISON exited the first turn in the lead with NOTRE DAME, PRIDE OF PAY 'n PAK and ATLAS VAN LINES following in close pursuit and MISS TIMEX trailing. So evenly matched were the first four boats, they appeared as one long continuous roostertail down the first backstretch.

MISS MADISON finished the initial lap one fifth of a second ahead of PAY 'n PAK and two fifths of a second ahead of NOTRE DAME with Billy Sterett, Jr. As the boats went through the first turn of lap two, MISS MADISON started to pull away, while PAY 'n PAK dueled with NOTRE DAME. The PAK moved away from Sterett on the second backstretch as NOTRE DAME lost power and slowed to a crawl. Schumacher tried to challenge front-running McCormick but, in so doing, blew his engine and went dead in the water.

Meanwhile, ATLAS VAN LINES had gone past the ailing NOTRE DAME and then moved into second place. By this time, MISS MADISON had an enormous lead and was putting added distance between herself and the ATLAS. Jim McCormick was flat out-driving his more powerful and heavily financed rival. Now no longer considered an upset threat to win, the U-6 was making it all look easy.

At the checkered flag, MISS MADISON had a full 22-second lead over ATLAS VAN LINES. Then came NOTRE DAME, followed by MISS TIMEX, which was lapped by MISS MADISON on the leader's last time around the course.

Jim McCormick's winning finish at Tri-Cities.

In winning the Atomic Cup, MISS MADISON became the first Tri-Cities champion to do the honors with an Allison engine as opposed to a Rolls-Royce Merlin. MISS MADISON also became the first Allison powered craft since 1966 to score consecutive race victories in the Unlimited Class.

"This is really sweet," beamed a jubilant McCormick. "This should prove to some race fans that our Gold Cup win wasn't a fluke."

Jim McCormick Wins The Tri-Cities Atomic Cup

The MISS MADISON team's triumph was now complete. "We're number one.", they proudly proclaimed. At long last, they stood at the very top of the racing world. In a sport dominated by millionaire owners and large corporate sponsorships, no one could afford to take the low budget U-6 for granted on the race course any longer.

Many years have come and gone since those brief shining moments in July, 1971, when MISS MADISON found her place in the annals of boat racing history and legend. To this day, she remains one of the most popular champions of all time.

Following her back-to-back victories on the Ohio and Columbia Rivers, MISS MADISON competed in three more races. She blew an engine and didn't finish at Seattle but quickly regained her commendable form at Dexter, Oregon, where MISS MADISON took a strong second place to PRIDE OF PAY 'n PAK, the experimental craft that had finally gotten its act together.

The PAY 'n PAK was not significantly faster on the

Madison -- Hydroplane Heritage - Fred Farley & Ron Harsin

straightaway than the other top Unlimited hydroplanes of post-1950 vintage. But, with her low profile/wide afterplane design, the PAK could corner more efficiently than any previous boat. Handled by Billy Schumacher, PRIDE OF PAY 'n PAK became the first to reach a speed of 121 mph on a 3-mile course at the 1971 Seattle Seafair Regatta.

The boat of the future had arrived as the first in a new and faster generation of Thunderboats. The handwriting was on the wall. Within two years, every boat would have to be a PAY 'n PAK design to be competitive.

In the twinkling of an eye, MISS MADISON was obsolete. The days of the box-shaped hull with the narrow transom and the shovel-nosed bow were gone forever. The craft that had debuted so many years earlier as NITROGEN TOO had seen its better days. It was time to make way for the new generation of world class race boats.

On the last day of her career, September 26, 1971, MISS MADISON took an overall third in the ATLAS VAN LINES Trophy Race at Lake Dallas, Texas, with a victory in Heat 2-A over Season High Point winner MISS BUDWEISER. The U-6 also tied down enough points to secure second place in the 1971 National Standings and thereby duplicated her 1964 accomplishment for overall performance during the season.

MISS MADISON's year-end box score read 26 heats started, 24 finished, six in first place, thirteen in second, four in third and one in fourth. This brought her all-time career total to an unprecedented 163 heats started, an even 150 finished, 26 in first place, 53 in second, 46 in third, 21 in fourth, 3 in fifth and 1 in sixth.

During the finale at Lake Dallas, the MISS MADISON deck started to work itself loose. McCormick kept her going at a safe conservative pace, finished the heat and brought the aging U-6 back to the dock for the last time.

A new MISS MADISON represented the Ohio River

town on the Unlimited tour, starting in 1972. Another MISS MADISON carried on the tradition, beginning in 1978, followed by another in 1988. While each of these boats represented their 13,000 owners well, it is still the 1963-71 hull that inspires awe.

When the new breed of Unlimited Class competitors take to the water, MISS MADISON, the Gold Cup Champion, will not be at the starting line with her engine roaring and roostertail flying. Presently owned by Dr. Ken Muscatel, MISS MADISON is scheduled for restoration by the U-6 crew and others who honor the memory of July 4, 1971.

MISS MADISON's racing days are over. But her fame will endure.

MISS MADISON - 1971 Gold Cup Winner.

Madison -- Hydroplane Heritage - Fred Farley & Ron Harsin

1971 Madison Gold Cup Race Statistics

1971 APBA GOLD CUP
Madison, Indiana - July 4, 1971
Length of lap: 2-1/2 miles - Length of heat: 15 miles
Length of race: 60 miles - Venue: Ohio River

FINAL STANDINGS POINTS
1. U-6 MISS MADISON, Jim McCormick 1400
2. U-70 ATLAS VAN LINES II, Terry Sterett 1400
3. U-25 PRIDE OF PAY 'n PAK, Billy Schumacher 1038
4. U-1 MISS BUDWEISER, Dean Chenoweth 925
5. U-5 TOWNE CLUB, Fred Alter 827
6. U-71 ATLAS VAN LINES I, Bill Muncey 625
7. U-7 NOTRE DAME, Billy Sterett, Jr. 619
8. U-8 MISS TIMEX, Ron Larsen 563
x U-32 HALLMARK HOMES, Leif Borgersen 000
x U-4 THE SMOOTHER MOVER, Bob Miller 000
x U-75 MISS MIAMI, Lou Nuta, Jr. Did Not Qualify

HEAT 1-A
1. ATLAS VAN LINES I 103.191; 2. PRIDE OF PAY 'n PAK 98.110; 3. NOTRE DAME 96.445;
MISS BUDWEISER and HALLMARK HOMES (sank) did not finish.

HEAT 1-B
1. ATLAS VAN LINES II 95.322; 2. MISS MADISON 93.296; 3. TOWNE CLUB 90.695;
4. Miss Timex 84.759; THE SMOOTHER MOVER (sank) did not start.

HEAT 2-A

1. PRIDE OF PAY 'n PAK 99.100; 2. ATLAS VAN LINES II 97.455; 3. TOWNE CLUB 93.555;
4. Miss Timex 86.289.

HEAT 2-B
1. MISS MADISON 99.356; 2. MISS BUDWEISER 96.791;
3. ATLAS VAN LINES I 93.717;
4. NOTRE DAME 86.110.

HEAT 3-A
1. MISS BUDWEISER 93.766; 2. TOWNE CLUB 92.386; 3. Miss Timex 86.455;
ATLAS VAN LINES I (sank) did not finish.

HEAT 3-B
1. ATLAS VAN LINES II 100.278; 2. MISS MADISON 99.907; 3. NOTRE DAME 96.239;
4. PRIDE OF PAY 'n PAK, time not taken.

FINAL HEAT
1. MISS MADISON 101.522; 2. ATLAS VAN LINES II 98.504; 3. MISS BUDWEISER 97.139;
4. PRIDE OF PAY 'n PAK 93.945; 5. TOWNE CLUB 91.231.
WINNER: U-6 MISS MADISON. Owner-City of Madison, Indiana.
Driver-Jim McCormick. - Team Manager-Tony Steinhardt.Crew-Bobby Humphrey, Dave Stewart, Keith Hand, Russ Willey, Harry Volpi and Everett Adams. Designer & Builder-Les Staudacher.

QUALIFICATION (2-LAP) AVERAGES:
1. ATLAS VAN LINES I - 110.159
2. NOTRE DAME - 106.888
3. HALLMARK HOMES - 105.696
4. PRIDE OF PAY 'n PAK - 104.895

5. MISS BUDWEISER - 104.784
6. ATLAS VAN LINES II - 104.469
7. MISS MADISON - 99.668
8. THE SMOOTHER MOVER - 99.393
9. TOWNE CLUB - 96.517
10. MISS TIMEX - 96.419

Jim McCormick

Driver of the MISS MADISON in the 1971 Gold Cup Race.

Jim McCormick drove the MISS MADISON (U-6) during the 1966, 1969, 1970 and 1971 racing seasons. In 1967, he drove for NOTRE DAME (U-7) and WAYFARERS CLUB LADY (U-19). In 1968, he piloted ATLAS VAN LINES (U-35) and HARRAH'S CLUB (U-3). During the Western half of the 1969 season, Jim drove ATLAS VAN LINES (U-19).

In mid-season 1971, Jim started an Unlimited team of his own. He purchased the former PARCO'S O-RING MISS (U-8) and ran it as MISS TIMEX, although he finished the season as driver of the MISS MADISON, while Ron Larsen handled the U-8.

In 1972, he campaigned two boats the MISS TIMEX (U-44) and the MISS TIMEX II (U-8) and drove the U-44 himself. In 1973, he owned and drove two boats, the RED MAN (U-8) and the RED MAN II (U-81).

RED MAN

While attempting to qualify the U-81 at Miami in 1974, the boat hooked in a turn and McCormick was thrown out. Jim suffered a serious leg injury, which left him with a lifelong limp. His relief driver, George "Skipp" Walther, was killed a few days later when the U-81 lost a rudder during a qualification run at Miami Marine Stadium.

McCormick returned to the driver's seat of the U-81 for the last two races of the 1974 season, taking a fifth at Madison, IN and a fourth at Jacksonville, FL.

In 1975, Jim briefly piloted Dave Heerensperger's PAY 'n PAK (U-1) but retired from racing after a third-place finish in the President's Cup. McCormick honored a previous commitment to campaign the U-81 (as OWENSBORO'S OWN) at his hometown Owensboro Regatta in 1975 but relinquished the cockpit to Howie Benns for that race.

Jim took one last sentimental journey as an Unlimited driver when he piloted the U-81, renamed SANTA RITA HOMES, at the 1977 Owensboro Regatta, where he finished eighth.

Following his retirement from competition, McCormick suffered health problems and was for a time (in 1981) legally blind.

Following laser surgery, which partially restored his eyesight, McCormick returned to the sport one more time in 1988 as co-owner with Bob Fendler of the POCKET SAVERS PLUS (U-4), driven by Steve David.

Between 1966 and 1977, Jim McCormick participated in a total of 70 Unlimited races and finished in the top three at 19 of them.

First Place
1971 - APBA Gold Cup/Indiana Governor's Cup - MISS MADISON - Madison, IN

1971 - Atomic Cup - MISS MADISON - Tri-Cities, WA

Second Place
1969 - Seafair Trophy - ATLAS VAN LINES - Seattle, WA

1971 - Champion Spark Plug Regatta - MISS MADISON - Miami, FL

1971 - President's Cup - MISS MADISON - Washington, DC

Third Place
1966 - Suncoast Cup - MISS MADISON - Miami, FL
967 - Atomic Cup - WAYFARERS CLUB LADY - Tri-Cities, WA

Madison -- Hydroplane Heritage - Fred Farley & Ron Harsin

1968 - Arizona Governor's Cup - HARRAH'S CLUB - Phoenix, AZ

1969 - Indiana Governor's Cup - MISS MADISON - Madison, IN

1969 - APBA Gold Cup - ATLAS VAN LINES - San Diego, CA

1970 - Atomic Cup - MISS MADISON - Tri-Cities, WA

1970 - APBA Gold Cup - MISS MADISON - San Diego, CA

1971 - Kentucky Governor's Cup - MISS MADISON - Owensboro, KY

1971 - Emerald Cup - MISS MADISON - Dexter, OR

1971 - ATLAS VAN LINES Trophy - MISS MADISON - Lake Dallas, TX

1973 - Champion Spark Plug Regatta - RED MAN - Miami, FL

1973 - Kentucky Governor's Cup - RED MAN - Owensboro, KY

1973 - National Champions Regatta - RED MAN II - Detroit, MI

1975 - President's Cup - PAY 'n PAK - Washington, DC

Madison -- Hydroplane Heritage - Fred Farley & Ron Harsin

"GENTLEMAN JIM"
Jim McCormick
1933 to 1995
A MADISON LEGEND
110

Miss Madison
U-6
RACING TEAM

Artwork contributed by Jim Lilly

Madison -- Hydroplane Heritage - Fred Farley & Ron Harsin

The 1971 Gold Cup Victory Photo

The Victory Photo - Jim McCormick, 1971 Madison Regatta Queen Carol Eggeman, Guy Lombardo, Indiana Govenor Edgar Whitcomb.

1971 Crew Tony Steinhardt, Bob Humphrey, Dave Stewart, Keith Hand and Russ Willey.

Consultants were Harry Volpi and Everett Adams of the former HARRAH'S CLUB Hydroplane Crew.

Madison -- Hydroplane Heritage - Fred Farley & Ron Harsin

Harry Volpi

Bob Humphrey, Tony Steinhardt and Graham Heath

Madison -- Hydroplane Heritage - Fred Farley & Ron Harsin

The 1971 Gold Cup Race Hydroplanes & Drivers

Terry Sterett - ATLAS VAN LINES II driver

ATLAS VAN LINES II - Finished 2nd in 1971 Gold Cup race.

Madison -- Hydroplane Heritage - Fred Farley & Ron Harsin

Billy Schumacher - PRIDE OF PAY 'n PAK driver

PRIDE OF PAY 'n PAK - Crossed the finish line in 4th, however, placed 3rd by points.

Madison -- Hydroplane Heritage - Fred Farley & Ron Harsin

Dean Chenoweth - MISS BUDWEISER driver

MISS BUDWEISER - Crossed the finish line in 3rd, however, placed 4th by points.

Madison -- Hydroplane Heritage - Fred Farley & Ron Harsin

Fred Alter - TOWNE CLUB driver. The only 1971 race driver that participated in the filming of the movie.

TOWNE CLUB - Finished 5th in the 1971 Gold Cup race

Madison -- Hydroplane Heritage - Fred Farley & Ron Harsin

Billy Sterett, Jr. - NOTRE DAME driver

NOTRE DAME

Bill Muncey - Driver of the ATLAS VAN LINES I

ATLAS VAN LINES I - Sank during 1971 Gold Cup race competition.

Madison -- Hydroplane Heritage - Fred Farley & Ron Harsin

Leif Borgersen - HALLMARK HOMES driver

HALLMARK HOMES - Sank during 1971 Gold Cup race competition.

Madison -- Hydroplane Heritage - Fred Farley & Ron Harsin

Bob Miller - THE SMOOTHER MOVER driver

THE SMOOTHER MOVER - Sank during 1971 Gold Cup race competition.

Madison -- Hydroplane Heritage - Fred Farley & Ron Harsin

Ron Larsen - MISS TIMEX driver.

*MISS TIMEX - Driver - Ron Larsen
Owner - Jim McCormick*

Madison -- Hydroplane Heritage - Fred Farley & Ron Harsin

Jim McCormick had purchased the MISS TIMEX just before the 1971 Gold Cup Race. Initially, his brother Roger McCormick had been scheduled to drive. However, when race day arrived, Ron Larsen was in the driver's seat.

The 1971 Race Winners

1971 NATIONAL CHAMPION MISS BUDWEISER - DEAN CHENOWETH

Miami - MISS BUDWEISER, Driver - Dean Chenoweth

Washington DC - ATLAS VAN LINES I, Driver - Bill Muncey

Owensboro - ATLAS VAN LINES I, Driver - Bill Muncey

Detroit - MISS BUDWEISER, Driver - Dean Chenoweth

Madison (Gold Cup) - MISS MADISON, Driver - Jim McCormick

Tri-Cities - MISS MADISON, Driver - Jim McCormick

Seattle - PRIDE OF PAY 'n PAK, Driver - Billy Schumacher

Eugene - PRIDE OF PAY 'n PAK, Driver - Billy Schumacher

Dallas - PRIDE OF PAY 'n PAK, Driver - Billy Schumacher

Madison -- Hydroplane Heritage - Fred Farley & Ron Harsin

1971 Madison Regatta Items

The above logo was used on the advertising flyers for the 1971 Gold Cup race. The colors were yellow lettering on a blue background.

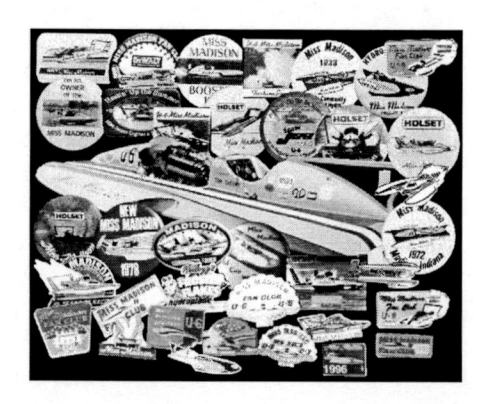

Many metal badges as well as other items have been created over the years by the hydroplane teams. These items have become collectors' items with some rare items becoming quite financially valuable. A few of these collectors' items are pictured here.

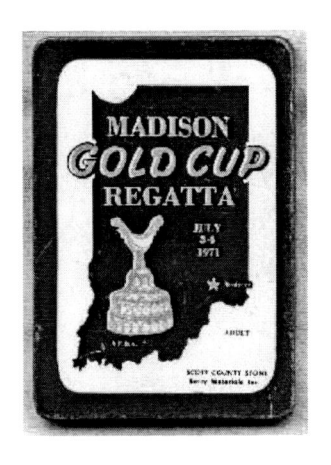

Madison -- Hydroplane Heritage - Fred Farley & Ron Harsin

1971 Gold Cup Adult Admission Badge

The movie showed a young Mike McCormick selling admission tickets to the 1971 Gold Cup race. In reality, the metal admission badge was used to enter the race site.

1971 Gold Cup Pennant

Madison -- Hydroplane Heritage - Fred Farley & Ron Harsin

1971 Gold Cup Child Admission Badge

Madison -- Hydroplane Heritage - *Fred Farley & Ron Harsin*

*Limited Edition Badge
Given only to the 1971 Gold Cup
MISS MADISON Crew Members.*

Madison -- Hydroplane Heritage - Fred Farley & Ron Harsin

Chapter Nine
More Madison Regatta

A collectors auto license plate for the car

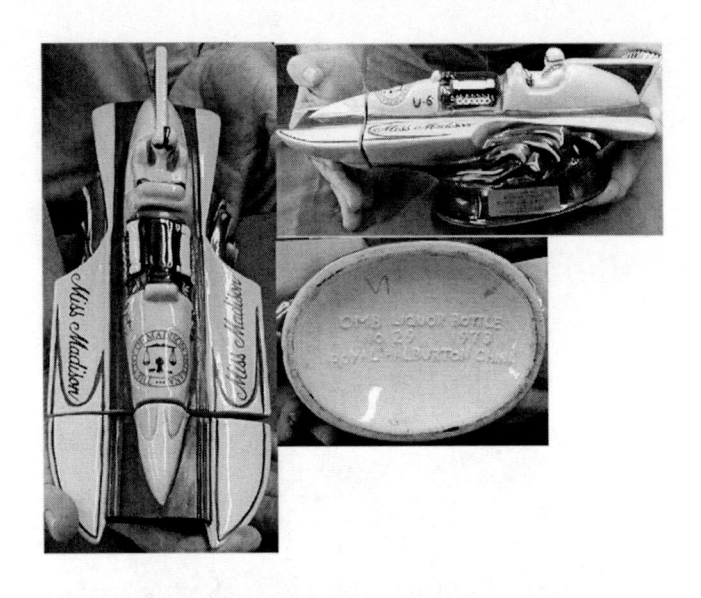

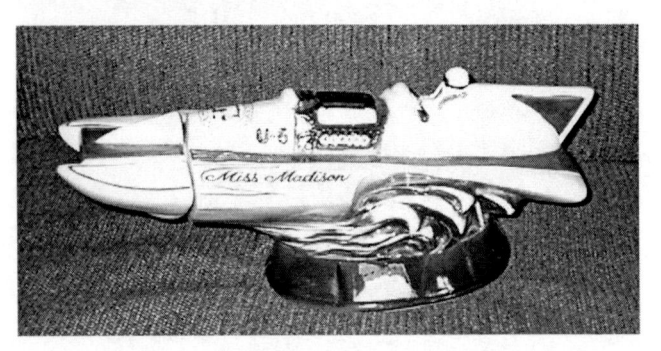

Madison -- Hydroplane Heritage - Fred Farley & Ron Harsin

This whiskey decanter was issued in a limited quantity. The collector value is well over $100.00 in excellent condition.

Madison -- Hydroplane Heritage - Fred Farley & Ron Harsin

Madison Regatta Sights

This sign is above the entrance to the pit area at the Madison race site.

On race day, the small town of Madison (population 13,000) grows to nearly 100,000 as spectators arrive to see the hydroplane races.

Madison -- Hydroplane Heritage - Fred Farley & Ron Harsin

An aerial view of the Madison Regatta race fans

Madison -- Hydroplane Heritage - Fred Farley & Ron Harsin

Madison -- Hydroplane Heritage - *Fred Farley & Ron Harsin*

The Madison Regatta Judges Stand

Madison -- Hydroplane Heritage - Fred Farley & Ron Harsin

The Madison Regatta Pit Area

On a hot summer day around July 4th, most of the spectators dress accordingly, as you can see in the next few pictures.

Madison -- Hydroplane Heritage - Fred Farley & Ron Harsin

Madison -- Hydroplane Heritage - Fred Farley & Ron Harsin

Madison -- Hydroplane Heritage - Fred Farley & Ron Harsin

Even the vendors at the race site dress for the warm weather

The HOLSET MISS MADISON

Madison -- Hydroplane Heritage - *Fred Farley & Ron Harsin*

Over the years, the MISS MADISON has had to find sponsorship money from companies to support its racing efforts. The boat ran under several sponsor names as displayed over the following pages. We have included many of the sponsors of the Madison owned hydroplane, however, we realize that not all of the sponsors have been included in this book.

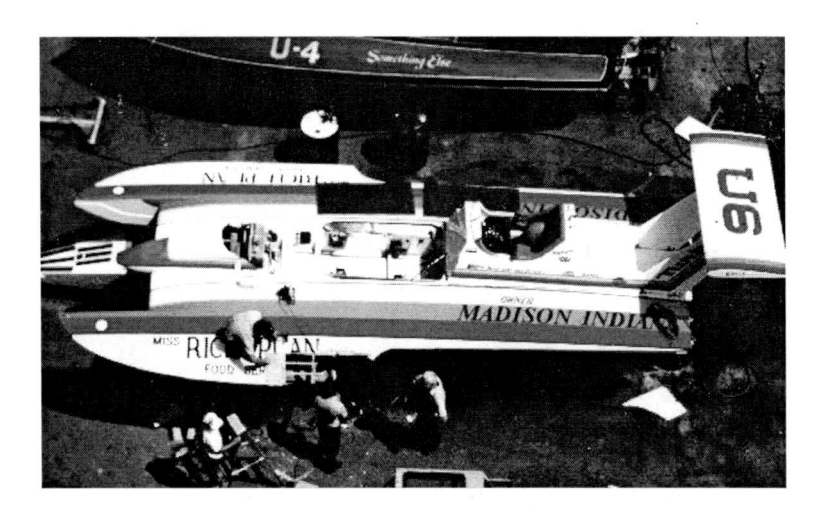

MISS RICH PLAN - MOBILE FOOD SERVICE

Madison -- Hydroplane Heritage - Fred Farley & Ron Harsin

The *AMERICAN SPEEDY PRINTING MISS MADISON*

MISS MADISON after a flip. Todd Yarling was driving and escaped uninjured.

Ky Yarling, (Todd's brother) said that the boat was towed to shore upside down. The canopy was open and the cockpit was filled with mud that required considerable removal before the boat could be inverted. Ky and others had to swim under the boat to remove the mud before the crane could lift the boat and flip it over.

Madison -- Hydroplane Heritage - Fred Farley & Ron Harsin

Photos of the KELLOG'S SUGAR FROSTED FLAKES "Tony The Tiger" MISS MADISON.

The current sponsor is OH BOY! OBERTO Beef Jerky

Madison -- Hydroplane Heritage - Fred Farley & Ron Harsin

At the end of the race day, most spectators leave immediately and never see the boats leave. Above is a picture of race fans in their boats leaving Madison after the race concluded.

Madison -- Hydroplane Heritage - Fred Farley & Ron Harsin

Other Hydroplanes That Have Called Madison Their Home

MASTER TIRE - Owned by Ed Cooper Sr. and Ed Cooper Jr.

MISS KENTUCKIANA PAVING

The former MY GYPSY was purchased by Graham Heath and "Wild" Bill Cantrell, it was sponsored by Jim Sedam, owner of the local business - Kentuckiana Paving.

Madison -- Hydroplane Heritage - Fred Farley & Ron Harsin

MISS TOST ASTI
After sponsoring the KENTUCKIANA PAVING, Jim Sedam purchased his own hydroplane and based his boat in nearby Hanover Indiana.

MISS BELLO'S PIZZA
Sponsored by the local Madison business Bello's Pizza

Madison -- Hydroplane Heritage - Fred Farley & Ron Harsin

Chapter Ten
Current Hydroplanes

The Current MISS MADISON

Current Driver: Steve David

Miss Madison Owners Representative: Bob Hughes
Team Manager: Charlie Grooms
Crew Members: Daryl Szymanski, John Leschinski, Pat Harris, Eric Bell, Greg Bentley, Richard Dunn, Greg Bredhold, Clint Hardy, Dennis Snyder, Robert Parks, Charlie McCluggage, David Shirley, Owen Blauman, Wayne Griffin, Matt Sontag, Randy Doughty, Tom Alfano, Randy Gayle, Charley Wiggins, Jason Lowrey, Mitch Moore, Dave Shepherd

Madison -- Hydroplane Heritage - Fred Farley & Ron Harsin

Steve David - Driver

Steve David - OH BOY! OBERTO (MISS MADISON) (U-6)

Home: Lighthouse, Florida

A prominent college teacher and Florida realtor, Steve David is also a lifelong boat racer, who is now in his third year of piloting the community-owned U-6.

The highlight of Steve's career was his triumph in the 2001 Madison Regatta on the Ohio River, after fighting off a persistent challenge from second-place Greg Hopp and ZNETIX in the Final Heat. This marked the first local win by the MISS MADISON team in 30 years (since 1971).

David's three other wins in the Unlimited Class were all with the Jim Harvey Motorsports team: Lewisville, Texas, and Honolulu, Hawaii, in 1993 and Kansas City, Missouri, in 1995.

Steve was Unlimited Rookie of the Year in 1988 with Jim McCormick's POCKET SAVERS PLUS.

He has over 250 race victories in the Limited ranks and over 500 heat wins.

Steve David is a past-President of the American Power Boat Association (in 1997-98).

Steve is the latest in a long line of MISS MADISON drivers since 1961. His predecessors include Marion Cooper, Buddy Byers, Jim McCormick, Milner Irvin, Jon Peddie, Ron Snyder, Mike Hanson and Todd Yarling.

Bob Hughes - Miss Madison Owners Representative

Bob Hughes has served as the president of the Miss Madison, Inc., Board of Directors for three decades. He was named Sportsman of the Year in 1983 by the Unlimited Racing Commission.

Madison -- Hydroplane Heritage - Fred Farley & Ron Harsin

Charlie Grooms - Team Manager

With over 20 years on the MISS MADISON team, Charlie Grooms started by washing parts when his uncle, Jon Peddie was named the team's driver in 1977. Over the years, Charlie graduated through the ranks to become team manager. As a volunteer, he oversees all aspects of the team including: boat set-up, race spotter, sponsorships, logistics, budgeting, personnel and other administrative duties. Charlie Grooms, a resident of Madison, is married with three children.

Madison -- Hydroplane Heritage - Fred Farley & Ron Harsin

2001 MADISON REGATTA

A Hollywood screenwriter could not have scripted a more popular outcome to the 2001 Madison Regatta. For the first time in 30 years, the community-owned boat took first-place before the hometown crowd.

MISS MADISON (disguised as OH BOY! OBERTO) and driver, Steve David, made a perfect on-the-nose start in the winner-take-all Final Heat, while three other boats "jumped the gun" and incurred a one-lap penalty.

For five heart-pounding laps, MISS MADISON held off a dynamic challenge from second-place ZNETIX and Greg Hopp, who forced David to work for it every inch of the way to the checkered flag and victory.

The front-page headline of THE MADISON COURIER, the following day, summed it all up in just two words: "Oh Boy!"

OH BOY! OBERTO Wins the 2001 Indiana Govenor's Cup

Madison -- Hydroplane Heritage - *Fred Farley & Ron Harsin*

The OH BOY! OBERTO Crew Victory Photo

OH BOY! OBERTO
Hydroplane Data:
Engine: Lycoming T-55/L-7
Horsepower: 2,650
Average Speed: 160 m.p.h.
Top Speed: 195 m.p.h.
Cockpit: F-16 Canopy
Shaft: 15,300 RPM
Compressor Ratio: 7:1
Weight: 6200 pounds
Fuel: 60 gallons / Jet A
Gear Box Oil Capacity: 5 gallons
Gearbox: 45% reduction
Length: 31 feet
Width: 14 feet, 6 inches
Propeller: 3 Blade, 26" Pitch-16" Diameter, Stainless Steel
Construction Materials: Honeycomb aluminum & fiberglass

Madison -- Hydroplane Heritage - Fred Farley & Ron Harsin

While the boat has had various sponsors over the years, the local citizens of Madison, Indiana, still call the boat the MISS MADISON. It is occasionally referred to as the MISS MADISON on racing telecasts. We residents of Madison are very proud of "our boat" and hope it continues to be an ambassador of goodwill, representing our community for many years to come.

Congratulations from the residents of Madison, Indiana to the OH BOY! OBERTO boat and crew for your 2001 Indiana Governors Cup win.

Winter In The Boat Shop

The truck sits outside waiting for racing season

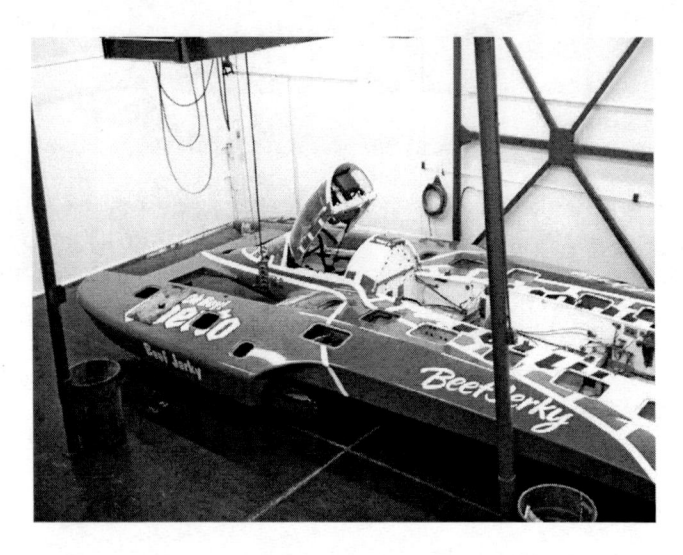

The turbine engine has been removed from the hydroplane racing hull.

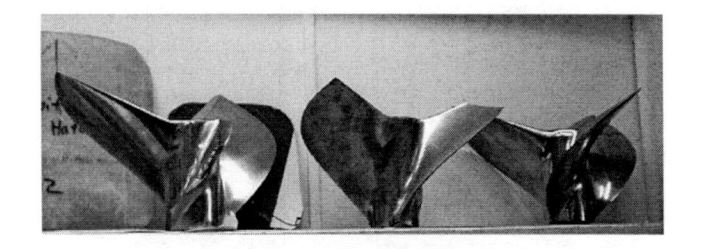

Three of the boat's propellers.

The turbine engine in the process of repairs.

The fuel injection system from the turbine engine.

The internal blades from the turbine engine.

Madison -- Hydroplane Heritage - Fred Farley & Ron Harsin

Miscellaneous parts for the turbine engine.

Madison -- Hydroplane Heritage - Fred Farley & Ron Harsin

MISS MADISON trophies on display at the boat shop

Madison -- Hydroplane Heritage - Fred Farley & Ron Harsin

Current Hydroplanes & Drivers

Madison -- Hydroplane Heritage - Fred Farley & Ron Harsin

Greg Hopp
Driver for the Leland Racing Team

LELAND RACING (U-100)

Madison -- Hydroplane Heritage - Fred Farley & Ron Harsin

Home: Snohomish, Washington

Greg Hopp, the son of racing veteran Jerry Hopp, made his Unlimited hydroplane debut in 1998 at age 30, but the story begins long before.

At age 9, Greg raced J Stock Outboards and finished second in APBA Region 10 High Points. He went on to drive in the A Stock, 1-Litre and 2.5-Litre Stock Limited classes. For many years, he served as a crew member on boats his father drove.

For his first full season of Unlimited activity, Greg borrowed a hull from Fred Leland. Operating on a modest budget, Hopp finished third in the National High Point Drivers Standings. Moreover, he became the first rookie in Unlimited history to earn more than 10,000 points during the season. Greg was an obvious choice for Rookie of the Year in 1999.

An employee of the Boeing Company when not racing boats, Hopp is best remembered by Madison Regatta fans for his second-place finish with ZNETIX (U-100) in the 2001 Indiana Governor's Cup. Greg gave spirited chase to the winner, Steve David and OH BOY! OBERTO (MISS MADISON), all the way in the winner-take-all Final Heat.

Madison -- Hydroplane Heritage - Fred Farley & Ron Harsin

Mark Evans
Driver of the U-8 LLUMAR WINDOW FILM

LLUMAR WINDOW FILM (U-8)

Madison -- Hydroplane Heritage - Fred Farley & Ron Harsin

Home: Redmond, Washington

Popular Mark Evans returns to Unlimited hydroplane racing in 2003 after a two-year absence as driver of Bill Wurster's newly acquired LLUMAR WINDOW FILM (U-8). This is the rebuilt version of a hull that Mark briefly drove in 1995 as the MISS BUDWEISER.

Evans started in his first heat of Unlimited competition at Detroit, Michigan, in 1991 as pilot of Ron Jones, Jr.'s AMERICAN SPIRIT. In his third race with the Jones team, Mark won the Indiana Governor's Cup at the 1991 Madison Regatta.

His best season to date is 1997, when he drove Fred Leland's PICO AMERICAN DREAM to four wins in a row. By far the most impressive performance by Evans and the PICO that year occurred at Seattle. After winning Heat 1-B, Mark flipped upside down in Heat 2-A. Evans was uninjured and rebounded to win the Final Heat.

Never before in the history of Unlimited racing has a driver flipped a boat upside down and come back to win the race, all on the same day.

Mark's brother, Mitch Evans, drives the MASTER TIRE (U-3) for owners Ed Cooper, Sr. and Ed Cooper, Jr.

Madison -- Hydroplane Heritage - Fred Farley & Ron Harsin

*Mitch Evans
Driver of the U-3 MASTER TIRE*

MASTER TIRE (U-3)

Home: Chelan, Washington

One of two racing Evans brothers, Mitch Evans first attempted to qualify as an Unlimited hydroplane driver in 1980 at the wheel of KW3 RADIO, an automotive powered boat, owned by his friend Rick Bowles.

Evans has spent most of his Unlimited career with Ed Cooper's U-3 racing team, starting in 1987. Mitch won the 1989 Tri-Cities (Washington) Columbia Cup race with COOPER'S EXPRESS. In 1991, Evans set the world piston lap speed record at 147.953 and raised it to 148.410 in 1995 with a turbocharged Allison.

He spent several years with the turbine-powered APPIAN JERONIMO team and finished second in the 1997 APBA Gold Cup at Detroit. In 1998, he was runner-up in the races at San Diego and Las Vegas.

In 2002, Mitch shocked the racing world when he raised the piston lap record to 160.370 with the new Cooper-owned VACATIONVILLE.COM (U-3) and led the field for two laps in the Final Heat at San Diego.

At the 2003 "Thunder On The Ohio" in Evansville, Indiana, under the sponsorship of MASTER TIRE, Evans guided the Allison-powered Cooper craft to a storybook triumph by defeating second-place Mike Hanson and the turbine-powered MISS WABX.. This was the first victory in the Unlimited Class by a piston boat in 14 years.

His father, the late Norm Evans, raced Unlimiteds between 1956 and 1970.

Madison -- Hydroplane Heritage - Fred Farley & Ron Harsin

*Mike Hanson
Driver of the U-9 Jones Racing Team*

MISS BELLO'S PIZZA (U-9)

Home: Bonney Lake, Washington

Nicknamed the "Boat Doctor," Michael D. Hanson is one of hydroplane racing's most versatile participants. He builds them and drives them.

Mike is best known to Madison, Indiana, fans for his ten-year stint with the community-owned MISS MADISON team between 1988 and 1998.

Hanson qualified as an Unlimited driver at the 1986 Tri-Cities (Washington) Columbia Cup with Fred Leland's U-100, an unsponsored craft with the generic name "BOAT" painted on it.

One of his best seasons was 1993 when he and the MISS MADISON (sponsored by KELLOGG'S FROSTED FLAKES) finished second in National High Points and first in the Star Mart Cup on San Diego's Mission Bay.

Mike has three other victories in the Unlimited Class: the 1994 Texas Hydrofest at Lewisville with MISS BUDWEISER, the 2001 APBA Gold Cup at Detroit with TUBBY'S GRILLED SUBMARINES and the 2002 Bill Muncey Cup at San Diego with SUN HARBOR MORTGAGE.

During the winter of 2003, Mike and his brother Larry Hanson spent a month in Madison modifying the MISS MADISON to help his former mount be more competitive.

Madison -- Hydroplane Heritage - Fred Farley & Ron Harsin

Dr. Ken Muscatel
Owner/Driver of the U-25 Superior Racing Team

SUPERIOR RACING (U-25)

Home: Seattle, Washington

Unlimited racing's only forensic psychologist, Dr. Ken Muscatel was a successful 6-Lite Class inboard pilot before stepping up to the Unlimited ranks. As driver of Bob Fendler's JACKPOT FOOD MART, Ken was Rookie of the Year in 1991. He started his own Unlimited team in 1993.

Along with his duties as owner/driver of the U-25, Muscatel served as APBA Unlimited Commissioner from 1998 to 2000 and as President of the Hydroplane and Raceboat Museum in Seattle from 1991 to 2002. He owns and drives several vintage hydroplanes, including Gar Wood's MISS AMERICA VIII, the replica HAWAII KAI III and the Gold Cup-winning MISS MADISON.

Ken's highest finish as an Unlimited hydroplane driver is a second-place in the 1998 Madison Regatta as driver of MISS NORTHWEST UNLIMITEDS.

At the 2002 Tri-Cities (Washington) Columbia Cup, Muscatel survived a horrific crash when the U-25 blew over backwards and literally broke into two pieces. Thanks to the F-16 safety canopy, Ken was uninjured. He leased a replacement hull from Fred Leland and drove it the following weekend in the Seattle Seafair Regatta.

Madison -- Hydroplane Heritage - Fred Farley & Ron Harsin

*Nate Brown
Driver of the U-16 MISS E-LAM PLUS*

MISS E-LAM PLUS (U-16)

Madison -- Hydroplane Heritage - Fred Farley & Ron Harsin

Home: Preston, Washington

A boat racer for 23 of his 44 years, Nate Brown pilots the Ellstrom family's "big orange machine." To date, he has four first-place trophies on the shelf.

In 2001, Brown captured the General Motors Cup at his hometown Seattle Seafair Regatta. He followed this with a triumph in the 2001 Bill Muncey Cup on San Diego's Mission Bay.

In 2002, Nate and MISS E-LAM PLUS claimed the Indiana Governor's Cup at Madison and the Tri-Cities (Washington) Columbia Cup and finished second in National High Points.

Brown landed his first Unlimited ride in 1992 with the Fred Leland team and was honored as Rookie-of-the-Year.

More recently, he took over the driving duties for the MISS MADISON (OH BOY! OBERTO) in 2000 after the retirement of Charley Wiggins.

When not racing hydroplanes, Nate runs his own business, Preston Performance Marine, which repairs and re-manufactures all description of boats for dealers and private clients throughout the Pacific Northwest.

Madison -- Hydroplane Heritage - Fred Farley & Ron Harsin

*Terry Troxell
Driver of the U-2 MISS TRENDWEST*

MISS TRENDWEST (U-2)

Home: Gig Harbor, Washington

A graphic artist by profession, a boat racer by avocation, Terry Troxell has been handling high-speed hydroplanes for 35 years. He is the new driver for 2003 of Jim Harvey's MISS TRENDWEST.

A two-time inductee into the prestigious APBA Hall of Champions for Limited inboard racing in 1997 and 1998, Troxell accepted his first Unlimited Class assignment in 2000 with the Fred Leland team.

Terry's career highlight to date is a victory in the 2001 Tri-Cities (Washington) Columbia Cup with ZNETIX II when he outran second-place Dave Villwock and MISS BUDWEISER by six seconds in the Final Heat.

Troxell had the satisfaction of winning at the same race site where he had qualified as an Unlimited driver the year before.

Terry's 2002 season highlights included second-place finishes at Evansville (Indiana), Madison (Indiana) and Detroit (Michigan) with Leland's variously named U-99 entry.

Troxell is related by marriage to the racing Weber family. His three brother-in-laws (Mike, Mark and Steve Weber) all drive power boats.

Madison -- Hydroplane Heritage - Fred Farley & Ron Harsin

Dave Villwock
Driver of the U-12 MISS BUDWEISER

MISS BUDWEISER (U-12)

Home: Seattle, Washington

Defending world driving champion Dave Villwock returns to the cockpit of the MISS BUDWEISER for the seventh consecutive year in 2003. Villwock also serves as team manager.

In the words of MISS BUDWEISER owner Joe Little, "I have been personally involved with many of the drivers for the MISS BUDWEISER over the years. I have to say that Dave Villwock truly has a passion for winning and being the best. He might not always have the fastest boat in the field, but he always finds a way to make it happen. Dave has proven that he is a true champion."

Joe reflects the words of his late father Bernie Little, who stated at the end of the 2002 campaign, "I've had some really great drivers and great crews over the past 40 years. But my current team is definitely the best. I know that Dave and his crew will always get the job done."

The 2002 season was a banner year for Villwock and the MISS BUDWEISER. They won three out of six races and accumulated 836 points in the O'Doul's High Point Championship Standings. This compares to 759 for second-place Nate Brown and MISS E-LAM PLUS and 709 for third-place Mike Hanson and SUN HARBOR MORTGAGE.

This brought Dave's victory total as an Unlimited hydroplane driver to 39, the highest among currently active Unlimited pilots. Only the late Bill Muncey (with 62) and the retired Chip Hanauer (with 61) have more wins than Villwock.

Madison -- Hydroplane Heritage - Fred Farley & Ron Harsin

*Mike Weber
Driver of the U-10 MISS EMCOR*

MISS EMCOR (U-10)

Home: Dawsonville, Georgia

Mike Weber drove his first Unlimited hydroplane race in 1997 at the Las Vegas Cup on Lake Mead with Mike Jones's MISS EXIDE.

Weber started racing Limited hydroplanes in 1977 at age 17 but took time out to earn a bachelor's degree from Western Michigan University in preparation for a career in the automotive industry.

Mike was 1998 Unlimited Rookie of the Year with the Jones team. He spent most of 1999 with Ed Cooper's MASTER TIRE and in 2002 succeeded his brother Mark Weber as the primary driver for Kim Gregory's MISS EMCOR.

At the 1999 Tri-Cities (Washington) Columbia Cup, Mike had the opportunity to step into the MISS PICO as relief driver for the injured Chip Hanauer. Weber finished second to Dave Villwock in MISS BUDWEISER and ahead of third-place, brother, Mark in YORK INTERNATIONAL. This was the first time that Mike and Mark had raced against each other in the Unlimiteds with competitive equipment. Mike averaged 140.829, while Mark did 138.956.

Madison -- Hydroplane Heritage - Fred Farley & Ron Harsin

Steve David
Driver of the U-6 OH BOY! OBERTO

Driver of the OH BOY! OBERTO (U6 - MISS MADISON), Steve David's information can be found elsewhere in this book.

Madison -- Hydroplane Heritage - Fred Farley & Ron Harsin

When Accidents Happen

Madison -- Hydroplane Heritage - Fred Farley & Ron Harsin

Amazing, this boat did NOT flip. It leveled out and, like a bird, flew above the water before coming down and continuing the race.

Madison -- Hydroplane Heritage - Fred Farley & Ron Harsin

The MISS BUDWEISER did flip.

And again

Madison -- Hydroplane Heritage - Fred Farley & Ron Harsin

MISS MADISON flips

CELLULAR ONE

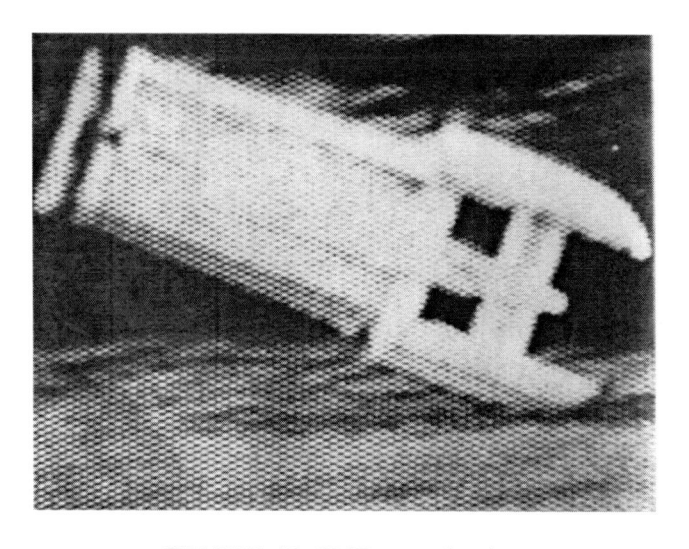

Madison -- Hydroplane Heritage - Fred Farley & Ron Harsin

CELLULAR ONE cartwheeling

Pieces of the CELLULAR ONE sponson

Madison -- Hydroplane Heritage - Fred Farley & Ron Harsin

The CELLULAR ONE and the MISS MADISON. First time published photos of the CELLULAR ONE wreckage (1987).

The CELLULAR ONE being placed on its trailer

Madison -- Hydroplane Heritage - Fred Farley & Ron Harsin

The flip in the 1987 Madison Regatta nearly claimed the life of, now retired, Steve Reynolds. The canopy saved his life.

The world would have been a darker place. Bless you Steve for staying with us.

Madison -- Hydroplane Heritage - Fred Farley & Ron Harsin

Hydroplane Radio Frequencies

U-1 MISS BUDWEISER 457.1375
U-1 MISS BUDWEISER 469.525
U-1 MISS BUDWEISER 469.575
U-1 MISS BUDWEISER 491.350
U-2 HARVEY MOTORSPORTS 469.225
U-3 MILL BAY CASINO 461.725
U-3 MILL BAY CASINO 464.725
U-6 MISS MADISON (OH BOY! OBERTO) 463.7125
U-6 MISS MADISON (OH BOY! OBERTO) 461.7125
U-7 MISS COST LESS CARPETS 467.100
U-8 LYNWOOD HONDA 460.000
U-10 SMOKIN' JOE'S 467.875
U-10 SMOKIN' JOE'S 468.475
U-14 COMPUTERS & APPLICATIONS 467.100
U-50 --- 461.650
U-55 --- 463.650
U-99.9 WELLNESS PLAN 464.425
U100/U98 PICO AMERICAN DREAM 464.8125
U100/U98 PICO AMERICAN DREAM 466.7125
Hydro-Prop Officials 464.550
APBA Private Channel 464.1375
Rescue 156.975

Using a portable programmable police scanner, you can listen in on the "behind the scenes conversations" at the hydroplane races. Any UHF scanner will work. Program the frequencies and listened to all of the action.

The Hydro-Prop Officials are a good one to listen to, especially with the flag start, because they tell the boats to "cut through", "lineup" etc.

The boat names change when they acquire new sponsors, however, the frequencies assigned by the F.C.C.

remain the same. These frequencies should provide listening enjoyment for years to come.

Almost all of these frequencies were working in Detroit, Evansville and Madison races, 2003.

Internet URL's of Interest

Unlimited Hydroplane Organizations

Hydro-Prop, Inc.
http://www.hydroprop.com/
Hydro-Prop Hydros (Unlimiteds)
http://www.hydroprop.com/hydros/
Hydro-Prop Formula One PROP
http://www.hydroprop.com/formulaoneprop/
American Powerboat Association
http://www.apba.org/
ULHRA (Unlimited Lights)
http://www.ulhra.org/

Unlimited Hydro Teams

U1 MISS BUDWEISER
http://www.budweiser.com/sports/ind_racing.html
U2 JIM HARVEY MOTOR SPORTS
http://www.jimharveymotorsportsinc.com/
U6 MISS MADISON
http://www.missmadison.com/
U8 LLUMAR Hydroplane Race Team
http://www.u-8hydro.com/
U9 JONES RACING Team
http://www.u9jonesracing.com/
U10 Unlimited Hydroplane
http://www.usaracingpartners.com/
U25 SUPERIOR RACING Team

http://www.superior-racing.com/
U28 NEW KID IN TOWN
http://www.unlimitedhydros.com/
U100 ZNETIX
http://www.web-visuals.com/znetix/

History

Fred Farley Hydro-Prop Official Historian
http://www.hydroprop.com/history.htm
Antique Boat Museum
http://www.abm.org/default.htm
APBA Historical Society
http://www.apbahistoricalsociety.org/
APBA Unlimited Hydro History
http://www.apba.org/categories/unlimited/history.html
Hydroplane and Raceboat Museum
http://www.thunderboats.org/
Mariner's Museum
http://www.mariner.org/
Motorsports Hall of Fame
http://www.mshf.com/
Through the Years: Madison Regatta Winners
http://revolution.3-cities.com/~mcelroy/madison.html

Hydro-Prop Race Sites

Evansville
http://www.thunderfest.com/
Madison
http://www.madisonregatta.com/
San Diego
http://www.bayfair.com/
Sanford
http://www.excitementinsanford.com/

Saskatoon
http://www.f1boatracing.com/
Seattle
http://www.seafair.com/
Tri-Cities
http://www.columbiacup.com/

Radio

Madison, IN WORX 96.7 FM
http://www.worxradio.com/
Tri-Cities, WA KONA 610 AM
http://www.konaradio.com/

Race Site Cams

Evansville River Cam
http://web.myinky.com/rivercam/
Hawaii's Pearl Harbor Cam
http://www.dohc.com/aloha/
San Diego Bay Cam
http://live.net/sandiego/
San Diego Mission Bay Beach Cam
http://www.bahiahotel.com/bah-webcam.html

Madison, Hanover & Jefferson County, Indiana Internet Links

Business Links

Key West Shrimp House
http://www.keywestshrimphouse.com
American Antiquities: Antique America
http://www.americanantiquities.com/madison.html
The Madison Mall

http://www.madisonindiana.com
Venture Out Business Center
http://www.vobc.com
Burleson Auction Company
http://www.oldmadison.com/auction
Bed and Breakfasts in Madison Indiana
http://www.roomsplus.com/bb/in/m/inm10045.htm
Inns and B&B's in Madison Indiana
http://www.inns.com/midwest/in014.htm
Historic Broadway Hotel & Tavern
http://www.oldmadison.com/broadway
The Thomas Family Winery
http://info.aes.purdue.edu/AgResearch/winegrape/Thomas_Family_Winery.html
Main Street Antique Mall
http://www.oldmadison.com/mainstmall
The Designing Woman of Madison
http://www.oldmadison.com/dwoman
The Attic
http://members.tripod.com/~theattic
Schussler House - Bed & Breakfast
http://www.the-mid-west-web.com/schussler.htm
Spring House Bed and Breakfast
http://www.the-mid-west-web.com/springhouse.htm
Clifty Creek Art Gallery
http://www.cliftycreek.com

Entertainment Links

Hydroplane Winners from Madison Indiana
http://revolution.3-cities.com/~mcelroy/madison.html
Ben Schroeder Saddle Tree Co. Museum
http://www.imh.org/imh/saddle/home.html
Sunrise Falls Municipal Golf Course
http://features.yahoo.com/golfcourses/in/madison/06624.html

Madison -- Hydroplane Heritage - Fred Farley & Ron Harsin

Miss Madison Hydroplane
http://www.win.net/~finsleft
Madison Regatta
http://www.seidata.com/regatta
Clifty Falls State Park
http://www.state.in.us/dnr/statepar/parks/clifty/clifty.htm

Government Links

Madison Chamber of Commerce
http://www.madisonchamber.com
Madison Indiana Main Street Program
http://www.seidata.com/~mainstre
Big Oaks National Wildlife Refuge
http://midwest.fws.gov/bigoaks

Media Links

The Madison Courier
http://www.madisoncourier.com
Roundabout Madison
http://www.roundaboutmadison.com/madison/index.html

Miscellaneous Links

Hanover Indiana Home Page
http://www.geocities.com/Heartland/Valley/1904
Madison Port Authority
http://www.madrr.com
Madison Indiana News
http://www.newquestcity.com/cities/IN/news/1310.htm
Madison Indiana Events Calendar
http://www.seidata.com/~madison1/events
Heritage Trail of Madison
http://www.seidata.com/~tpritch
Madison Area Convention & Visitors Bureau

Madison -- Hydroplane Heritage - *Fred Farley & Ron Harsin*

http://www.seidata.com/~madison1
Madison Indiana
http://www.seidata.com/~madison
Historic Madison Indiana
http://www.oldmadison.com
Madison
http://www.madison.com
Madison Indiana Official Site
http://visitmadison.org
Madison City Guide
http://www.oldmadison.com/cityguid.html
Historic Madison Inc.
http://www.imh.org/imh/saddle/home.html
Historic Hoosier Hills
http://www.hhhills.org/index.html

Tornado Links

It may seem strange to some individuals that there would be links to tornado sites within this book. On April 3rd, 1974 the communities of Madison and Hanover Indiana, (along with most of Jefferson County), were devastated by a killer tornado and several smaller tornadoes.

The Madison Regatta was cancelled and most race fans never arrived at Madison in July, while the local communities were attempting to recover from the damage.

Therefore, most of those race fans never saw the destruction that caused the cancellation of the Madison Regatta. This regatta was later rescheduled and run in October of that year. For many fans, the damage can be seen here for the first time.

The links show graphic photos of the tornadoes' destruction.

Madison Tornado Pictures

http://www.april31974.com/images/Madisonintornadophotos.html

Hanover Tornado Pictures

http://www.april31974.com/images/Hanoverintornadophotos.html
April 3, 1974 Tornado Site
http://www.april31974.com/index.html

Note: Internet URL's come and go. The links listed in this section were active at the time of publication.

Madison -- Hydroplane Heritage - Fred Farley & Ron Harsin

*The Ohio River
A dull cessation of yesterday's
Paddlewheelers and coal barges
Churning bygone days for hydroplanes...*

Madison -- Hydroplane Heritage - Fred Farley & Ron Harsin

Books published by
Bristol Fashion Publications
Free catalog, phone 1-800-478-7147

Boat Repair Made Easy — Haul Out
Written By John P. Kaufman

Boat Repair Made Easy — Finishes
Written By John P. Kaufman

Boat Repair Made Easy — Systems
Written By John P. Kaufman

Boat Repair Made Easy — Engines
Written By John P. Kaufman

Standard Ship's Log
Designed By John P. Kaufman

Large Ship's Log
Designed By John P. Kaufman

Custom Ship's Log
Designed By John P. Kaufman

Designing Power & Sail
Written By Arthur Edmunds

Building A Fiberglass Boat
Written By Arthur Edmunds

Buying A Great Boat
Written By Arthur Edmunds

Boater's Book of Nautical Terms
Written By David S. Yetman

Practical Seamanship
Written By David S. Yetman

Captain Jack's Basic Navigation
Written By Jack I. Davis

Creating Comfort Afloat
Written By Janet Groene

Living Aboard
Written By Janet Groene

Racing The Ice To Cape Horn
Written By Frank Guernsey & Cy Zoerner

Marine Weather Forecasting
Written By J. Frank Brumbaugh

Complete Guide To Gasoline Marine Engines
Written By John Fleming

Complete Guide To Outboard Engines
Written By John Fleming

Complete Guide To Diesel Marine Engines
Written By John Fleming

Trouble Shooting Gasoline Marine Engines
Written By John Fleming

Skipper's Handbook
Written By Robert S. Grossman

Madison -- Hydroplane Heritage - Fred Farley & Ron Harsin

White Squall - The Last Voyage Of Albatross
Written By Richard E. Langford

Cruising South
What to Expect Along The ICW
Written By Joan Healy

Electronics Aboard
Written By Stephen Fishman

Five Against The Sea
A True Story of Courage & Survival
Written By Ron Arias

Scuttlebutt
Seafaring History & Lore
Written By Captain John Guest USCG Ret.

Cruising The South Pacific
Written By Douglas Austin

After Forty Years
How To Avoid The Pitfalls of Boating
Written By David Wheeler

Catch of The Day
How To Catch, Clean & Cook It
Written By Carla Johnson

VHF Marine radio Handbook
Written By Mike Whitehead

About The Authors

Fred Farley
The Official APBA./Hydro-Prop Historian

Fred Farley has been a college instructor and a writer for many years. Fred has written articles for Hydro-Prop, the American Power Boat Association, various newspapers and hydroplane racing magazines and many of the websites found on the internet.

For over 30 years, he has held the position of the "Official Historian" for the "big boats", (the Unlimited hydroplanes) and he provides stats whenever needed by radio, tv, or officials at any race site.

Fred served as a consultant to the "MADISON" movie, providing information to the movie makers about the different hydroplanes and the 1971 Madison Gold Cup Regatta. As a

Madison -- Hydroplane Heritage - *Fred Farley & Ron Harsin*

writer, a historian and as a consultant, there is no one more qualified to write about the actual events that surrounded the race that was the inspiration for the "MADISON" movie.

Having known Jim McCormick, his son Mike and many of the MISS MADISON crew members personally, Fred can provide more than just the "facts and figures." He can tell you about the people...who they really are.

Originally from Seattle Washington, Fred and his wife Carol moved to just outside the city limits of Madison, Indiana, where they have made their residence for the last several years.

Ron Harsin
Certified Computer Information Specialist

Ron Harsin has a background as a computer consultant to companies like IBM, Motorola, General Motors, TRW and Ameritech. The jobs have included a variety of tasks including programming, technical writing, applications testing, systems administration, systems engineering design and project management. Ron also served as a college instructor teaching computer software courses.

As a technical writer, Ron has several published technical documents and manuals created for the computer industry. The writing experience helped considerably with the development of this book.

Ron is also an accomplished BMI affiliated songwriter with several songs recorded by different artists as well as a published photographer.

Ron, his wife Ilene, daughter Jennifer and son Randy are life-long residents of the Madison, Indiana, community and spend each year caught up in the Madison Regatta activities.

Madison -- Hydroplane Heritage - *Fred Farley & Ron Harsin*